Praise for *A Death in Brazil*:

'An astonishing feat of storytelling' Peter Carey, Booker Prize winner

'Glorious ... fascinating and revealing' *New York Times*

'Robb paints a picture of Brazil quite unlike any other' *Publishing News*

'Electrifying ... enthralling' *Literary Review*

'Fabulous ... Robb writes beautifully' *Irish Examiner*

'Reads like a thriller' *Daily Express*

'Eclectic and inventive ... a wonderful book' *Guardian*

'A brilliant portrait of Brazil' *Sunday Tribune*

'Fabulous ... an utter marvel' *Waterstone's Books Quarterly*

'An intoxicating cocktail of a book' *Time Out*

'Masterful' *Sunday Business Post*

'A brilliantly atmospheric study of twenty-first-century Brazil' *Sunday Times*

'Excellent ... mesmeric ... I eagerly anticipate Robb's next work' *Irish Times*

A DEATH IN BRAZIL

A DEATH IN BRAZIL

A Book of Omissions

PETER ROBB

BLOOMSBURY

First published in Great Britain in 2004
This paperback edition published in 2005

Maps copyright © by Alex Snellgrove

A CIP catalogue record for this book
is available from the British Library

Bloomsbury Publishing Plc, 36 Soho Square, London W1D 3QY

ISBN 0 7475 7316 6
9780747573166

10 9 8 7 6 5 4 3

All papers used by Bloomsbury Publishing are natural,
recyclable products made from wood grown in well-managed forests.
The manufacturing processes conform to the
environmental regulations of the country of origin.

Printed by Clays Ltd, St Ives plc

www.bloomsbury.com

IM

Florisvaldo Azevedo de Carvalho

You can put anything into a book of omissions. Reading one of these never worries me at all. What I do when I get to the end is close my eyes and think of all the things I didn't find in it. So many great ideas come to me then, really deep thoughts.

—MACHADO DE ASSIS

The tram goes by full of legs:
White legs, black legs, yellow legs.
My God, what are all the legs for, asks my heart.
But my eyes
ask nothing at all.

—CARLOS DRUMMOND DE ANDRADE

Brazil made me intelligent.

—FERNAND BRAUDEL

Contents

The maps of Brazil (pp. xii and xiii), which have been drawn by Alex Snellgrove, show only places mentioned in the following pages. Likewise, the notes on reading and the chronology at the end refer only to matters discussed in the book.

The tilde over a Portuguese vowel, as in *São Paulo* or *sertões,* stands for a missing *n* at the end and means the sound comes out through the nose. The sound of an *nh* pairing in a Portuguese word is that of an *ñ* in Spanish or *gn* in Italian—so the surname of *Euclides da Cunha* rhymes with *vicuña* in Spanish and *prugna* in Italian.

The currency values that appear here, many of which are necessarily approximate, are expressed in United States dollars valued at the time of the transactions they refer to. So after ten or more years, PC's billion would be a lot more today.

Like everyone, I went to Brazil to get away. At the start it was easy. At the beginning of the eighties Brazil still had a consulate in Naples. It occupied a vast and gloomy suite with high ceilings and the finest veil of dust in a distinguished Umbertine palazzo two blocks in from the Bay of Naples. On a clear day you saw Capri from its window. The consulate was marked by an oval plaque in burnished brass and you reached the office in a clanking iron cage lift with glowing mahogany seats.

Reception was manned by a tall lady with parchment skin and horn-rimmed glasses on looping chains. Another nearly identical lady lurked within. They wore silk blouses in the heat and cashmere twinsets in the cool. Their dark straight hair was pulled severely back, their feet shod in costly lace-up shoes and they moved softly in long skirts of handwoven tweed. Behind frosted glass yet farther in I once saw a fuzzy silhouette of the consul himself. There was a huge old Underwood typewriter with a cast-iron frame on the reception desk, several wilting aspidistras in pots in the corners and a fly spotted schoolroom map of the Americas on the wall.

I wondered what the old ladies had to do in Naples, and they seemed to be wondering too. There was a Brazilian I knew study-ing navigation at the Naval Institute, but that was all. A hundred years earlier, hundreds of thousands of southern Italian peasants had sailed steerage for Brazil from Naples. Now a third of Brazil-ians were of Italian descent, and some of the richest among them. The rich came to Italy to spend and poor Brazilians, if they could, would come to Italy to make their fortune. Most of these were transsexuals who plied their trade at the richer freeway junctions farther north. The Naples consulate was dying of inanition. The fan flicked around noiselessly. Though they made it clear that the consul couldn't be hurried, the two ladies were always very good about my visa. Of course I went to Rio first, via Casablanca with Royal Air Maroc, which had a special offer at the time.

I

Mixed Blood

_____

Murders happen anywhere and mine most nearly happened in Rio. Twenty years later only the scar of a small knife wound on my arm reminds me that this is a memory and not a dream. The night went on and on like a dream, with a dream's ungraspable logic, or a Brazilian soap's. Details become wonderfully vivid, like the old carving knife with a long curved and darkened blade carelessly left earlier on the kitchen bench of the Copacabana flat, in the moment it was being held at my throat. My Portuguese lost its rudimentary awkwardness and became unreally fluent very fast. Words I'd never known I knew came pouring from my throat. Things flowed with a dream's weightless speed. The danger lay in the speed. A flailing knife blade moves faster than thought. Movement had to be slowed, the heat lowered. It was the one thing I understood. Let nothing happen. Respond to violence, speed and noise not with violence, speed and noise but with ponderous torpidity, envelop each new threat in slowness. The beautiful Portuguese periods began to roll, slowly, slowly, but with what baroque grace, from my amazing tongue. Obtuse fearlessness stayed the hand with the knife, impassive calm put a little wobble in the spin of violence.

Chance put the knife in Adelmo's way. Chance, or Brazilian entropy, had saved me a moment before we worked our way to the kitchen. The hideously old-fashioned Brazilian furniture, in the sitting room where it started, was a wasteful mass of dark stained solid tropical woods and dark brown cowhide upholstery and rows and rows of little brass studs. Adelmo grabbed a lamp and then a chair to smash my head. The lamp's base was cast iron and the chair too heavy to wield. When we got to the kitchen and he grabbed the knife, a tiny part of the first fatal impetus had been lost.

There—elaborately, ponderously, holding his eye hypnotically—I laid out the options. I told him that since he held the knife, if he wanted to kill me he probably could. Yet there was nothing of value in the flat. This looked likely. There were a couple of pairs of jeans and a few faded polo shirts flung around and that was all. The American dollars under the mattress would have been to Adelmo a huge amount, but I didn't mention them. If Adelmo started looking he would find the money in seconds and kill to leave with it. It was important that Adelmo's mind be kept off looking for cash. The baroque periods surged and crashed, like the thunder of surf in the night, as Adelmo learned that the noise of any assault would be heard by the neighbors in the next apartment. The neighbors, Adelmo heard in an elaborately inserted parenthesis, were close friends of mine. There were several of them next door, young, physically vigorous, and holders of a spare front door key to the apartment we were in. The apartment was vacant, but what was baroque prose for, if not to put a spin on simple realities? Finally, the doorman downstairs—armed of course, and a family friend—was the only person able, from within his reinforced glass booth, to activate the mechanism that unlocked the heavy glass doors that opened onto Our Lady of Copacabana Avenue, and the doorman had strict instructions never to let visitors out of the building unless they were accompanied by myself. A strange order, improbable even, but a slight cause for concern to anyone who might be planning to kill and leave. By name I mentioned the particularly hideous Rio jail where Adelmo would spend the rest of his life.

This little touch kicked in to great effect. Nobody likes to feel trapped, and Adelmo knew all too well the experience of being locked in. He hated it. Later, when the emotional cycle had turned again, he showed me the scars on his legs that had been made by the bullets fired at him by the reform school guards as he ran off. Adelmo had been fending for himself since he was very young. And for the next couple of hours he held the carving knife to me in the kitchen. And talked. He laid out his life in words. The flashing-eyed knife-waving anger dissolved in tears of unhappiness at his lot. The only reason he hadn't killed me, he said with an unexpected sob, was that I'd been so good to him. The restaurant, the respect. He would have killed anyone else. Then the knife was at my throat again. Still holding the knife, he threw his arms around me. *Kiss me,* he said, and I did. It was a very charged and prolonged kiss. The illusion of hieratic distance conjured by ornate prose suddenly vanished. *I already saved you tonight,* Adelmo said. *The guy on the bus was going to knife you.*

Very likely. As the juddering, madly speeding late night bus had swung and hurled us to our destination, a giant of a black man, an amazingly tall and muscular figure in running shorts and running shoes and a tank top, had been toward the end of the journey the only other passenger. He seemed to know Adelmo. They had talked apart for a while, and the stranger glanced across at me from time to time. *You didn't understand what we were saying,* Adelmo said now. *We were talking carioca slang. He wanted to roll you. He wanted to knife you and I said no.* What I remembered was that in one of his huge hands the black man was kneading, while he and Adelmo talked inaudibly, a rather finely made gold spectacle frame, an elderly person's spectacle frame. The lenses were gone, and his hand was reducing the frame to a tiny compact ball of twisted gold wire. I wondered what had happened to the owner of the glasses.

Adelmo didn't often get the chance to talk about himself and in those days I was a good listener, even without a knife at my throat. Adelmo was happy that, maybe for the first time in his life, he had an audience. Through all the moods and phases of the night, however, the kitchen knife was always there. Once, as if to remind me of my place, Adelmo slashed my arm with the knife. The cut wasn't deep but the flowing blood raised feelings of danger, violence and panic. *You'll tell them I attacked you.* Adelmo slashed his own arm and started bleeding too. He calmed down. *I'll tell them you knifed me first.* He was pleased at the logic of his self-wounding. The danger passed and he went back to telling me about himself, between declarations of love and spasms of murderous rage. We went on for hours, standing in the little kitchen. In the end we were clinging to each other and too exhausted to go on. We wiped off some of the sticky blood and went downstairs. The doorman hardly woke as he buzzed us out. The sky was getting lighter over the Atlantic.

I caught sight of Adelmo again the following night, crossing a square in the centre of Rio. He was hard to miss. He was wearing, at a very rakish tilt, a beret in shocking pink angora. It set off his virile features in a striking manner. He waved cheerfully and seemed on top of things again. It was the last time I saw him. I left a couple of days later and it was years before I went back to Rio. The night in the kitchen at Copacabana with the carving knife felt like the logical and personal conclusion of various other things I'd seen and experienced on that and earlier visits in the early eighties. It was hard not to feel that visiting Rio was asking for trouble. Things were starting to break apart in Rio. The signs were everywhere.

In that very building, the day I had rented the apartment a few months earlier, I came home to a foyer full of military police. One grabbed me and threw me against a wall and a couple of others began, not gently, to search me. Someone said, *That's not him,* and I was flung aside. Police were swarming all over the building. When I got upstairs, I glanced out of the window, which gave onto a kind of small enclosed garden. One or two stories below was a sloping roof that stopped at a wall on the garden. The wall was built up a little beyond the bottom of the roof to hide the slope, and in this gutter between roof and wall, partly hidden by some opulent green foliage, I was looking down on a poorly dressed black youth who was lying very low and very still. Later the police left and when I looked out again the boy was gone too.

Another time a boy raced barefoot across the promenade, the cycling track, the palm lined central island and the multiple traffic lanes of the Avenida Atlântica, away from the beach and heading for one of the transverse streets that led through Copacabana and, eventually, to the mountainside that rose behind the strip of apartment blocks, sheer out of the flat coastal strip, walls of rock, clefts of green. A watch bracelet was glinting in the boy's hand and the military police were shooting at him, and into the crowd on the footpath. They missed the boy, and the schoolchildren and housewives and street vendors and the people heading home from the beach and the taxi drivers talking and smoking while they waited for fares. The police didn't always miss, when they shot into a crowd of Brazilians.

The boy was making for the precarious jumble of shacks that clung to the rocky peaks. This was the *favela* and his home. In a reversal of the world's more usual urban growth, which had the hovels of the poor clustered at the base of green hills where the rich lived in their big houses, Rio's peculiarity had the twentieth-century apartments of the wealthy spread along the beachfronts—first of Guanabara Bay and then of the long ocean beaches to the south—while the unaccommodated poor, flooding to Rio from all over Brazil, made their flimsy homes on the breathtaking and dangerous heights of the monoliths looming over the concrete real estate. Shacks crashed into green crevasses with every downpour, but the view from Rio's favelas was stupendous. I climbed up once to look around, and found a pastoral settlement whose most dangerous inhabitant was a huge brown sow wandering its paths. Twenty years later, no outsider would dream of entering a favela without protection. The name of the favela came from a long way away. In the remote hinterland of Bahia in the Northeast of Brazil there was a rocky peak rising by a flat riverbed called Monte Favella. At the end of the previous century thousands of Brazilian troops had been sent from Rio and other places south on a terrible punitive expedition and they had camped on Monte Favella, which gave its name, after they came back, to the encampments of the poor on the spectacular hills of Rio. But it would be years before I learned what happened at Canudos, the place overlooked by Monte Favella.

One day, changing some of the Yankee dollars I had smuggled out of Italy, I was given twice as many greasy wads of big red *cruzeiro* notes as even the day's exchange rate warranted. The sheer distractedness about the value of money that Brazil's rate of monetary inflation promoted was another symptom of social breakdown that was almost as vivid as the children on the streets and the police shooting into crowds. The supermarkets of Rio were being looted in those days by people who left the money and took the sacks of beans and rice. Money in Brazil was something you dealt in fistfuls. You didn't bother to count it.

Brazilians were living through the long dragged out death of a military dictatorship that had lasted for nearly twenty years, though there was no sign then of an end to the agony of military rule. Brazil under the military had lacked the kind of drama that caught the world's interest. There had been none of Chile's bombing of the presidential palace, no murder of an elected leader, no massacres in the football stadium, no *caravan of death*. Neither had there been the disappearances of Argentina, the unmarked gray Ford Falcons, the unspeakable tortures, the still living bodies dropped into the sea from helicopters, the ignominy of a lost war in the South Atlantic. There was in Brazil no brilliantly sustained urban guerrilla resistance to match the exploits of Uruguay's Tupamaros, no permanent guerrilla army in the jungle like Colombia's or Peru's. For the world there was something dispersive in Brazil's hugeness, something that made it hard to focus on. When the Brazilian military had taken power a decade before the others, it happened so blandly that the world hardly noticed. The United States, poised between Kennedy's murder and the Vietnam War, prized stability and acquiescence in its hemispheric neighbors and thought military rule in Brazil would be a good thing, and so in 1964 did a lot of people in Brazil. The governor of Rio tried to rally the troops against their leaders, but he failed and followed the president into exile.

For years the military had it easy, riding Brazil's late and remarkable industrial boom, and the euphoria and pride that went on for years after Brasilia was built. The stunning modernist capital that went up almost overnight in the empty highlands of Brazil's very center projected a land of great resources and endless confidence. This and a little money and a lot of soap operas kept people's minds off who exactly was running the country and how they were doing it. There was resistance, however. Students were imprisoned. Foreign diplomats were kidnapped and exchanged for the prisoners, who were flown to safety in Cuba and Mexico while the Brazilian military looked foolish. More prisoners were taken. The screw turned in 1968. The military closed down the Congress altogether and began *a counterrevolution within a counterrevolution* in which murder and torture became routine instruments of the government's control. The resistance responded by kidnapping the American ambassador. Advised by great and powerful friends, Brazil's dictators developed the model of government that the military of Chile and Argentina would soon make their own. Subversives—who might be anyone who did not loudly acquiesce to the military— were hunted down. Most of Brazil's democratic leaders had already left the country.

Lacking an entire political class and the smartest and bravest of its younger generation, who were overseas or dead or vanished within the regime's prison system, Brazil was not well placed, after ten years of military rule, to deal with the drastic downward turn the world economy took in the 1970s. A few years of floundering and the less cruel and obtuse of the military wanted to tiptoe backward out of government, only not too precipitately, in case people noticed. Control without responsibility was what they wanted and never achieved. By the eighties the bankers and industrialists were despairing. There was no way Brazilian generals could manage one of the world's larger industrial economies, let alone avert at the same time a social disaster that only the boom had held off. Power was draining from the military, but still they were afraid to let go.

People were quietly coming back. There were amnesties. Unreported and unnoticed, particularly by holidaying foreigners with no desire at all to involve themselves in the travails of underdevelopment, things began to stir. In 1979 the movement produced a minuscule grouping of recently exiled and tortured intellectuals and some industrial workers who were raising their heads. Grandly, the little group called itself the Partido dos Trabalhadores, the Workers' Party. Late one afternoon I was on the Avenida Rio Branco, in the center of Rio, just as darkness fell. Down the splendid street, choked with buses and their black exhausts, and all the yellow VW Beetle taxis running on sugar-cane alcohol, marched a little procession of demonstrators. There were twenty of them at the most, and I think they were marching about education. They were carrying a red flag with a black star, as well as the banners. They seemed a tiny and frail looking group, determined but a bit intimidated, a lot less assertive in their persons than the messages on their banners, in danger of being crushed by the traffic and a general indifference. It was a surprise to see them in the brutal and hedonistic Rio de Janeiro of the last years of military rule. Their banners identified them as members of the Workers' Party. I wondered how long they would last. I wondered how they were able to exist at all in that Brazil, in Brazil as it was at the start of the eighties.

The desperation of some of the younger Brazilians—people like Adelmo, whose concentration on personal survival left little space for the big picture—was reflected in a film made around this time, a gritty and technically economical film that recalled De Sica's and Buñuel's images of another generation's lost children in Naples and Mexico. The new movie was called *Pixote* and was seen by a lot of people. I saw it in Rio, and watched the rather obvious back projections of Arpoador beach—which showed that the group of reform school fugitives from São Paulo have arrived in Rio—in a cinema that was a few hundred meters from the beach itself, the little kink between Copacabana and Ipanema, in full vibrant color with real bodies. *Pixote*'s young actors, in the true vein of neorealist art, were what they played, or near enough. The child who played Pixote, the pale and watchful youngest of the group, and the feeling center of the film, was an eleven-year-old from São Paulo. Fernando Ramos da Silva was the only one of the group who didn't quite live on the streets. He was one of a family of ten children from the industrial outskirts of São Paulo. His father was dead. Father and mother were country people from the Northeast who had come south to pick coffee and like so many others from the Northeast were sucked into the megalopolis of São Paulo, the biggest, richest, dirtiest and most dangerous city in South America. Mother and children survived by hawking lottery tickets on the streets.

A lot of people saw *Pixote* in Brazil and around the world, but not many doors opened for Fernando. He had a few small acting jobs, but he never really left the world of his origins. When he was seventeen he married a girl a year younger and they had a child. He had a few run-ins with the local military police, and he felt they picked on him because of the film. He felt typecast for life as a derelict and killer by his childhood role as *Pixote*. In 1987, when he was nineteen, he was playing cards at home when the military police raided the neighborhood. He hid at a neighbor's place, and when the police found him hiding under a bed they fired seven shots into him point-blank. They reported that Fernando had died while resisting arrest. There had been no charges against him. Because *Pixote* had been seen by millions of people, the death was picked up by the international wire services, and the Italian papers, who felt the news embodied either a confirmation of everything the film had foreshown or a bitter irony about the way art could take over a life. Which it did. Both readings were true, though in Brazil it was a very ordinary death, a death like thousands of others that were happening every year.

The deaths still happen. In 2003 another Brazilian film came out called *City of God,* which was the name of a Rio favela and the title of a novel by a young Brazilian writer called Paulo Lins, who had grown up in the City of God. From childhood he had lived through the City of God's fall from a quickie housing estate knocked up in the days of the military into the blood soaked stamping ground of the drug gangs who worked out of it. The drug gangs, winners and losers, living and dead, millionaires and foot soldiers, had been Paulo's childhood friends. His novel and the film enacted the spiral of violence and terror that all Rio's favelas have known in the last twenty years. Even more than in other countries, drugs are a growth industry in Brazil, which shares long and uncontrolled borders with all the biggest producers of cocaine. For several of these countries Brazil is both a vast market and their outlet to Europe and the world. Drugs are the only economic activity possible in the favelas but are not confined to the favelas. The drug runners of Rio now blow up cars, stop traffic and stop business in the smartest seafront suburbs. You would have to be a Brazilian to know what it means for Paulo Lins to have made it out of the favela and become a student, a poet, a researcher, an admired novelist, but the favela is pursuing him. The favela is overtaking Brazil.

The film of *City of God* has great visual flair, but it convinces, like *Pixote* twenty years before—if not as much as the novel— because its actors are real. And like the boy who played Pixote, the young actor who plays the boy who rises to control the favela's drug business has remained trapped in the world he came from. A few months after the film went around the world, he was arrested after a police chase along the beachfront in the smartest part of Rio. The teenager had made nothing out of his film and had a cocaine habit to feed. Like most of the other hundred or so who played in the film, he still lived in the favela. One of the actors became a model, a few got parts in a soap called *Women in Love,* a lot of them did a film workshop. Most of them were still living on hope rather than money. The film's director said that *to give these boys money . . . would only lead them back to cocaine addiction.* The violence of the drug business is a new mutation of the old, old violence of Brazil, which is a country of immense natural wealth, at peace with its neighbors and facing no unusual turbulence or social unrest within its borders. Yet the killing rate in Brazil, tens of thousands of violent deaths a year, falls within the parameters of the United Nations' definition of a low intensity civil war.

It was natural that a film about the lost children of Brazil's cities be played out along the narrow axis of Rio and São Paulo, which are only a few hundred kilometers apart. Everything in Brazil revolves around Rio and São Paulo and it has been like this for more than a hundred years. The building of Brasilia merely triangulated the airline traffic patterns. There is more money in the cities of the Southeast than anywhere else in Brazil, and more killing. Rio on Guanabara Bay sprawls over the habitable parts of the most beautiful site in the world. It was the slave and sugar city of the south, snatched from the French in its infancy and francophile to its marrow, the old capital of imperial Brazil, dazzling in its disease riddled belle époque, reimagined as the *marvelous city* of flying down to Rio and twentieth-century dreams of beaches, music, football, drugs and sex, ringed and overlooked and now increasingly invaded by its favelas. For the world, Rio goes on being Brazil.

São Paulo lacks Rio's splendor of place but it has the sex and drugs and the violence, a lot of money and even more people than money. A Jesuit mission station in the sixteenth century, inland from Portuguese coastal power and near the *índio* souls God wanted, for centuries it stayed a little inland cattle town. Its tough and cruel settler *bandeirantes* were the first Europeans to penetrate Brazil's interior on their long slaving forays against the índios. The hills around São Paulo were perfect for coffee shrubs and in the latter days of slavery São Paulo was transformed by money from the worldwide coffee boom. The European immigrants flooded in to replace the slaves. A million Italians, hundreds of thousands from Portugal, from Japan, from

Syria, from Germany, these were the first. São Paulo created and supplied its own demands, and when industry came to Brazil it came first to São Paulo. Now twenty million people make São Paulo maybe the fourth biggest human agglomeration on the planet. Rio is huge and lovely and terrifying. São Paulo is huger and more terrifying and not lovely at all. The immensely rich hover over the city's canyons in their own helicopters, fluttering at sunset between the corporate tower and the gated residence. São Paulo has more private helicopters than any other city in the world, more armored limousines, more armored ordinary cars, more armed security personnel and more desperate people than any other urban center on the face of the earth.

———

Seven years later, I got an early morning train to Rome and caught the afternoon flight to Lisbon. The Portuguese airline flew out of Lisbon at one in the morning and touched down in Recife at daybreak. Recife is nearly two and a half thousand kilometers north of Rio and the flight to Recife from Lisbon took a lot less time than any flight to Rio or São Paulo. It took me to another country. It took me to the Northeast—more exactly to the Northeast's oldest settled states, narrow Pernambuco and Bahia, which is bigger than France—and to a sense of the Brazilian past.

The Northeast is seen in Brazil as a problem. From its larger coastal cities, it can look very like the Southeast. The model is always Rio. There are the rows of high and shoddy new apartment blocks—each with the name of an Italian old master painter or a culturally prestigious place in France in wrought iron script on the fortress street-level wall—built along the Atlantic beaches at the edge of the city. They are the same in every coastal city in Brazil, and it is easy to forget for a moment which particular city they belong to. Which city you are in. Geography and architecture and climate are all equally unhelpful. The same vast resort hotels stand at every strategic point, always doing so much less business than they were built for and showing the same underpaid figures in uniform idling out front. But these appearances deceive. The Northeast is different.

The past is present in the Northeast. Rio and São Paulo destroy as they grow, but walk down certain streets in a northeastern city and you might be in the 1940s. There is the cream painted curved art deco cinema, with its turnstile and its popcorn vendors, there is the milk bar with stools and tropical milkshakes, there are the lean men with hats over their faces, asleep on the tray of a beat up old truck. Walk around a corner and slavery seems not to have ended. You see black women with huge bundles on their heads and shirtless men straining to move a two wheeled cart and not a car in sight. A bell clangs in the tower of a baroque church, the homeless clustered in its porch. A thin choir drones in the flimsy chapel of an evangelical sect.

Go through some tiny town of the northeastern outback. Pass the silent people on the stone front steps of their pastel washed and windowless one-room houses. The houses are built in rows along the beaten unpaved street, and along the beaten track a skinny mule pulls some sacks on a decrepit dray, and then a darker long eared mule ambles past under a barefoot boy in a big straw hat with a fraying brim. He's riding bareback with a slack rope halter resting in one hand, while the young girls with chairs and mirrors do each other's hair on the dusty verge. The narrow road that brought you there goes on forever, the hills undulate mildly until lost in the haze and if you lose yourself in the present you lose your bearings entirely. The interior of the Brazilian Northeast is a world apart—high, bare, hot and terribly dry. The coast of the Northeast is moist and lush and follows that eastward jutting shoulder of the South American continent that seeks the matching indentation in the west coast of tropical Africa. Recife is on the shoulder's easternmost bulge.

Recife was built on the islands of a river delta, where the Capibaribe River and the Beberibe and the Pina and the Tijipio and the Jordão all flowed into the Atlantic, under the protection of that slim but effective line of rocks that runs along the coastline a little way offshore. This was the crucial reef, the *arrecife* that gave the city its name and protected its shipping by breaking the force of the Atlantic swell. Recife had no splendid bay like those of Salvador and Rio, no dramatic cliffs or monolithic outcrops, just this stubborn little line of barely visible rocks. Recife didn't even have the amenity of a splendid green hill looking out over the Atlantic and cooled by ocean breeze. Olinda, the old capital, was built on such a hill. Olinda was adjacent to Recife, but still separate and special. The Portuguese had built Olinda in 1537 and it was one of the oldest settlements in Brazil, but in the early seventeenth century it had been knocked out by the Dutch. The Netherlands were scrabbling for a foothold in the continent, and clung for twenty years to a strip of coast in the Northeast. They were the people who had founded Recife a hundred years after Olinda. Caught in time, the old city of the landowners and the church stayed on its hill, run down and incomparably more beautiful, snatching at the crumbs of a hand to mouth tourism. From the middle of the seventeenth century Recife, with its merchant houses and its docks, was where the action was.

Where the bus tipped me out at first light, groggy from the Lisbon flight, was somewhere on the island of Santo Antônio. Guided by helpful hands, I stumbled into a small hotel whose modest entrance was hidden by a rank of yellow-canopied vendors' booths. It was called the Nassau, after Prince Maurits of Nassau, the man who founded Recife. The hotel was not large, but taller than the buildings around it, and taking coffee on the top floor you got an exhilarating oblique glimpse of hazy seafront and cobalt ocean in the morning sun, and a lungful of warm salt air. Nearer by was a confusion of baroque bell towers, domes, terracotta tiled roofs, and raw low-cost office blocks, their untreated concrete sides blighted by huge blotches of black tropical mold. The big avenue below was packed with rows of buses that were hardly moving, some little cars, and crowds of tiny people on foot, their foreshortened legs striding out very fast in every direction.

The footpaths teemed with people, and the streets were almost impassable from the number of hawkers' stands. The hotel was in a cobbled space called the Largo do Rosario, and the handsome church was at one end. A few yards away, in the wedge shaped space in front of Nossa Senhora do Carmo, lots of sellers had no stalls. They came from the country and spread their fruits on a cloth, little mounds of mangoes, little hands of delicate bananas, pyramids of limes, assortments of bell shaped *caju* fruit, pink and pale yellow, with the poisonous green *castanha* still attached, which when roasted would become a cashew nut. There were *cajá,* a kind of yellow plum, as well as *caju.* There were guavas and pawpaws and custard apples in small heaps. Most of the fruits had only their índio names. Sharp red *pitangas* and twigs of *pitombas* like clusters of suntanned Ping Pong balls. Women squatted with a pan of palm oil over a charcoal fire, frying *acarajé,* their African bean meal patties with a dried shrimp embedded in the top like a red jewel.

The mouse gray blanket of the rat poison man, positioned discreetly just around the corner, with its carefully arranged display of the mummified corpses of dozens of rodents dispatched by his product, always drew an absorbed knot of onlookers. Even more stopped to look at the anaconda writhing around the shoulders of the man selling barks and herbs and little bottles of his own special remedies. The herb vendor was an orator and a performance artist as much as a healer, and he and his snake held large crowds transfixed, until he paused to give them an opportunity to buy. Some of the pedestrian alleys were so jammed with the plywood stalls of watch repairers, vendors of coconut and banana and chocolate cake, or roast corn, or hot dogs, or combs and necklaces and wrist bands or used vinyl records, that you could hardly move. The jewelers— watch repairs and trinkets—had their own alley. Sellers of used comics and agricultural magazines, old physical culture reviews and odd encyclopedia volumes and other reading material concentrated in the literary area under the arcade of Avenida Guararapes by the Bar Savoy, where on Friday evenings a lady in her forties sang on the footpath with an electronic keyboard and snare drum player. The side alleys off the arcade were entirely given over to hot dogs and sticky cakes. The green coconut-juice stands stuck with the browsers along the arcades and the crowds jostling at the bus stops. The sellers of pencils, string, brown paper, envelopes, ballpoint pens and postcards had their own specialized stands over on the other side of the avenue around the post office steps. But anywhere at all in the city someone might be standing on the footpath by a tiny trestle table with a few choice digital watches, a heap of garlic, some coconut sweet, a luminous toy on a string or some objects of religious devotion.

A lot of the dense mass of people moving on foot through the city carried wares with them. Most of the crowd moved really fast, flinging out their legs and arms in a way only Recife people did when they had somewhere to go. People with something to sell were sometimes only semi-ambulatory, like the popcorn vendors and the hot dog men, who worked from big glass boxes mounted on bike wheels or pram wheels. The others traveled lighter and faster and were often underage. The newspaper sellers were emblazoned with the masthead colors of the

Diario de Pernambuco, the oldest paper in South America, and edited out of a stately nineteenth-century edifice near the Largo do Rosario, or its rival from a newer building around the corner, the modernizing *Jornal do Comercio.* The shoeshine boys lugged their heavy wooden boxes on a leather strap or a cruel rope over their shoulder and kept their eyes to the ground for those leather shoes striding along among the plastic flip-flops and the cheap runners. The shoeshines concentrated on the bars and restaurants, since sitting shoe leather was half the battle and after a few beers even better. Shoeshine was the most thankless job of all. The kids who stood around in the Praça do Carmo all day, leaning on a sign announcing *I buy gold,* had it easy.

The food sellers also hung around the bars. There were an awful lot of bars in Recife, a bar consisting largely of a few rickety folding tin tables and like chairs set up on an uneven footpath, and an awful lot of kids to service the hunger pangs that follow a few drinks. Toward the end of the afternoon the streets filled with boys carrying broomsticks over their shoulders. Around a nail at each end of the broomstick were suspended little plastic bags of *amendoim,* which were peanuts. They came raw or roasted or steamed, ready to shell or preshelled, in large bags or small. You could also buy cashew nuts and quails' eggs. Other children spent their evenings lugging little braziers around, made out of old paint tins and filled with glowing charcoal, like a church censer. In the other hand was a tray of long blocks of white cheese impaled on wooden skewers. Your skewer of cheese was grilled over the little brazier while you drank your beer and waited. The cheese was the Northeast's white *quiejo coalho,* made from curd. When darkness fell—and the sun dropped out of the sky in the space of a few minutes—the older youths arrived who had spent the day trudging along the sand at Boa Viagem with dishes of shrimps or buckets of oysters and now came to town to move what was still unsold.

Between the Largo do Rosario and the *Diario de Pernambuco*
was a small garden at the confluence of several streets around
which there were a lot of people gathered on account of the
many bus stops for the different lines. The small garden itself
was busy with the meeting and greeting of unattached ladies
and unattached gentlemen, who I noticed often left in pairs after
striking up an acquaintance. At one end a crowd had gathered
around a wiry middle-aged man with skin like finely polished
wood. He was wearing a black cowboy hat and dark glasses and
a very clean, slightly frayed, short-sleeved blue-and-white-check
cotton shirt and playing an old acoustic guitar that he had wired
up to a primitive and even older amplifier and a battered black
speaker box. He was thrumming the guitar and not so much
singing as chanting or intoning a long ballad that had the
bystanders gripped. Each strophe finished with a flourish and
the listeners laughed. I couldn't make out what he was singing
about in his hypnotic way. It seemed to go on forever, but the
singer knew how to hold an audience.

On the corner, a few yards away, another man was squatting
by a display of leaflets. There were dozens of them and they were
the words of songs like the one being sung. At once crude and
beautiful, the long rhymed ballads were hand-set in ancient
irregular letterpress, printed on folded sheets of the cheapest
pulp paper. Some of the libretti were laid out on the ground
and others were held up for sale on a frame strung with clothes-
lines, to which they were pegged and fluttering like drying
underwear or trapped birds, with a crude and vivid woodcut on
the cover. I bought half a dozen at a few cents each for their
gorgeous letterpress. Others might have wanted them for their
woodcuts. Music, story, image were here combined. I bought a
ballad about a girl who turned into a snake and another on the
arrival in hell of Lampião—the outback bandit who wore steel
rimmed glasses and an outback leather hat studded with silver

medallions, and was the greatest of the Northeast's primitive rebels. I unpegged the story of a boy who didn't know how to make love to girls and the account of a football match in purgatory. The black man and the rubber tapper. The boozer and the believer. Not quite Homer, or even Ovid, they had their moments. Newer songs fed into a repertory of workings and reworkings of favorite local themes, which was why a new take on the one-eyed Lampião was still a good bet fifty years after Lampião and his girlfriend and his men had been cut down in an ambush by the military police. The armies of type, poor and a bit ragged but impeccably in step, were marching now through pagelet after pagelet of newsprint already dry and yellowed under the piercing sun.

The bafflements of Recife derived from more than the clutter of its streets and the busyness of its traffickings. The flatness of the interlocking delta islands, and the network of mysterious waterways that cut across the reclaimed land, the number of similar but different bridges, made walking around town like covering the pieces of a big jigsaw puzzle. The lay of the land gave you no help and neither did the direction of the water flow, for the rivers were all tidal, and their waters ran both ways. I walked for hours on some early forays, convinced I was heading inland, only to end up on the waterfront on the island of São José, Recife's oldest part, where the old warehouses and the customs station and shipping offices clustered. This was a largely deserted and somewhat sinister place after nightfall but in the daytime you could get a man to row you out to the reef and pick you up later, and lovers used to do this. Beyond the reef, finally, there was nothing but the ocean and Africa.

———

Recife's streets had a strangely familiar feel. Their random intensities reminded me of Naples. They also recalled a book. Many

years before, on a wet day in Edinburgh, I had found a copy of
the first edition in English of Gilberto Freyre's *study in the development of Brazilian civilization . . . translated from the Portuguese of
the fourth and definitive Brazilian edition by Samuel Putnam,* as the
title page had it, bound in a black cloth like oilskin and published in New York by Alfred A. Knopf in 1946, thirteen years
after its original had first appeared in Brazil. In English it had
become *The Masters and the Slaves.* Freyre was a descendant of
sugar plantation owners and Recife was his city. In this first
book, which he wrote out of homesickness and published in
Brazil in the early 1930s, he described in sweeping generaliza-
tions and intricate, gripping detail the culture of the sugar plantations in colonial Brazil. The two poles of that culture, as the
title of his book made clear in Portuguese, were the *Casa-grande
& Senzala,* the big house of the white masters and the slave
quarters of the captive African workers. The piercing light, the
lush green of the fields of tall waving sugarcane, the cobalt ocean
off the coast, the humid heat and farther inland the bone dry
cruel clarity linked the Mediterranean culture of the masters and
the African cultures of the slaves and the tropical American culture of the displaced índios in the enclosed and isolated world
of the big sugar estates.

What linked the masters and the slaves was sex. In Freyre's
intricately documented study, every matter of life on the sugar
plantations led subtly back to sex. The sex was so deeply present
in his material that Freyre hardly needed to be explicit about it.
It was sex enhanced by the gorgeousness of the climate and the
sweetness of the sugar, and also sex made perverse by the cruel
relationship of masters to slaves, of the Roman Catholic Church
to African practices and indigenous forest life. Every new theme
he turned to became an aspect of sexual life. It was a very seductive picture of a slave society, a lot more complex in its reci-
procities than I had ever imagined. The Brazil of the sugar

plantations was, in Freyre's account of it, profoundly influenced by the values and practices the captives had brought with them from West Africa, so that in time the culture of the Portuguese masters had been subtly but radically transformed by the ways of the people they used as chattels. Brazil had turned into a society vastly different from that of the slave owning southern states of North America through the intimacy that existed on all levels between masters—and mistresses, and the children of the Portuguese masters and mistresses—and their slaves and their slaves' children. If in Protestant North America sex with slaves had been nasty, brutish, short and a matter of profound shame, particularly when the children were born, in the lax Catholic Brazil of the tropics, sex across the divide of race and ownership seemed to be at the very center of plantation life. Sometimes, reading Freyre, you wondered how they ever got the cane harvested and crushed and the juice boiled down.

In Freyre's view all this produced, over the four centuries and more of Portuguese settlement in Brazil, a much more fluid relationship between black and white than the English or North American or Spanish colonies ever knew. The Portuguese had been enthusiastic about sex with the índios too, until they had killed most of them off with their European diseases and their attempts to enslave and Christianize them. Brazil was peopled with black, whites, índios, and descendants of black and white, black and índio, índio and white, and endless further variants of the three as the generations passed. Sexual mixing laid the social ground for a benign equality in diversity of all Brazil's races and cultures, once the institution of slavery itself had dropped away, as it did at the end of the nineteenth century. By then the diversity was being enriched with a flood of Brazilians from other parts of Europe and from the Middle East and Asia. It was immensely seductive, Freyre's tropical pastoral of the vanished world of the sugar estates, conjured in sensuous and loving detail. Most seductive of all was the idea that out of Brazil's sensual and promiscuous past a new society had grown where the races flourished and racism was extinguished. The *new world in the tropics* that Gilberto Freyre wrote about so exuberantly and so prolifically in book after book was a marvelous dream.

To Brazilians in the 1930s the image Freyre held up of their own society had been quite startling. The Brazilians who shaped Brazilian institutions—the white Brazilians—had always lacked confidence in their racially bastard society. The blacks and the bastards were so many and the honorable white *fidalgos* so few. Even ordinary white people were not all that thick on the ground. There was nothing they could do about it. The solution, it seemed, might be to give up the idea of a ruling caste altogether—the idea Spanish America clung to—and go for modernization. In 1889, a year after she had formally abolished slavery in Brazil, Princess Isabel and her thoughtful and once astute but now elderly and infirm father, the emperor Dom Pedro II, who was now known around Rio as Pedro Bananas, were startled to find themselves escorted to the docks by the military, put on a boat and shoved off to Europe, where Pedro would die a couple of years later in a modest hotel in Paris. The army was in power. The Brazilian republic was proclaimed.

The republic's motto, *Order and Progress,* girdling the globe with the stars of the Southern Cross on Brazil's beautiful new green, blue and yellow flag, proclaimed its positivist values; and betrayed, in its very peremptory formulation, the new rulers' deep anxiety about their new body politic. It gave away their eminently military sense that keeping a tight grip on things was an even higher priority than moving things forward. The republicans were about control. Their aspirations were entirely European and in sweaty, chaotic, sensual Brazil, whose wildly oscillating economy was entirely based on export agriculture and controlled by the commodity markets of Europe, there was a lot to embarrass people who wanted Brazil to become a nation-state of a European or North American kind. The past was even more embarrassing than the present. Centuries of indiscriminate couplings had produced a people of bastard voluptuaries. If the positivists and the social Darwinists were right, and the founders of the republic of Brazil were convinced they were, Brazil was doomed to underdevelopment because so many Brazilians were inferior material. There was a terrible tension between the expansiveness and optimism that were generated in even the tightest mind by Brazil's gorgeous climate, its vastness and beauty and abundance, and the nagging fear of being doomed to backwardness.

When the nineteenth century ended Brazil was a little less entirely a society of the great landed estates, ruled by the sugar growers, the cattle growers, the rubber growers, the coffee growers. The cities were growing, especially the capital, Rio, and the new Brazilian republic was the creation of the city middle classes, the businesspeople and professionals who mediated between the landed barons and the rest of the world. The economy was booming and the city people of Brazil's belle époque were resolutely staring across the Atlantic for a glimpse of Europe, whence all the fine things came that they were now importing. Especially they were trying to make out France, which was entertaining its own unrealities at the time, like the rest of a Europe already drifting toward the Great War. Imported into the latterly slave society of tropical Brazil, the unrealities of the nineties boom blossomed with a heady luxuriance in Rio.

Then there was the world war and the world bust. For Brazil it was the crisis that ended the old republic and introduced—another new European fashion, in its way—the dictatorship of Getúlio Vargas in 1930 and its enhanced version, the New State, in 1937. It was into the newly uncertain Brazil of the early thirties, where the bust of world capitalism was no less amplified than the boom had been, that Gilberto Freyre's amazing book was born. It amazed everyone. It celebrated everything that the intellectuals of the new Brazil had been in deep denial about for fifty years: the bad old world of the slave plantations and their brutal, lustful patriarchal tyranny. It announced that out of this world, and specifically out of the sexual life of slave own-ing society, in the backward and embarrassing culture of the rural Northeast, the uniquely splendid civilization of Brazil had been born.

The paradoxes of Freyre's case were greatly perplexing for Brazilian intellectuals trying to make sense of their country's place in the modern world. Young Gilberto was barely thirty when he wrote *The Masters and the Slaves.* He had spent time in Europe and studied in the United States and maybe for this reason had no sense of inferiority about Brazil. His book was also disconcertingly well written, slangy and extravagant, exu-berantly, vividly particular and filled with the sights and smells and tastes of the Northeast. Gilberto's familiarity with the jokes and locutions of Brazil's illiterate masses, his knowingness about their social and culinary and sexual habits as well as their lan-guage, shattered decorum. Food and sex had never been held to be a part of culture at all, let alone considered with Gilberto's playful unadornment. It was especially startling to the guardians of ruling values that the entirely white and irreproachably fidalgo grandson of plantation masters should have been so familiar with the daily life of his social inferiors—it seemed like a betrayal of his class and race. Other Brazilians, and especially northeasterners like the young Jorge Amado, who was in his teens and already starting to write the popular life of northeast-ern Brazil into novels that would be read around the world, were simply dazzled. Never mind that most of its Brazilian readers knew nothing of the Northeast, let alone the long gone life of the old sugar estates. Brazilians recognized themselves in Gilberto's book. The verdict in the end, though it was a long time coming and never entirely unqualified—Gilberto Freyre has been in and out of favor over the years, and has a singular way of disconcerting both right and left—was Amado's, that *Gilberto's work leaves us all more Brazilian.* The unfamiliar pleasures of his style lowered resistance to his thesis and seduced his readers into embracing all the pleasures of a racially mixed Brazil.

Gilberto was a prolific writer, but none of his later work ever quite matched this first young man's book in its impact. He went on writing the same book over and over. There were two sequels—completing a massive trilogy on the uniqueness of Brazilian civilization—and a flurry of smaller books. Each new book was a variant reworking of the first, elaborating and embellishing its argument, and taking the story into his own time. All shared its marvelous sensitivity to the significance of the physical details, the concrete particulars that give the theory its seductive life. Fat footnotes thrust their way up every page, stories nested within the stories of the principal narrative like the *Arabian Nights,* under the guise of additional facts. The current Brazilian edition—the forty-second—unwisely confines these to the end of each chapter, whereas the splendid design of Knopf's put them in legible double columns at the foot of the pages they often occupy almost entirely. Freyre's translator, Samuel Putnam, was even more irrepressibly devoted to the footnote than the master himself, and his own further notes were interspersed with and sometimes added to and qualified Freyre's own. The reader had to make his own way through their typographical luxuriance.

Gilberto Freyre was not an ideas man. He snatched at whatever looked useful—or even merely interesting—and worked it into his tale. A later Brazilian anthropologist complained that

Gilberto always compromised his findings by intruding a novelist's touch. He didn't mention the readiness to draw support from some of the cracker-barrel racists, mad phrenologists and weird theorists of the psychosexual who were pullulating in the twenties and thirties, the mental sludge of the very positivism Gilberto's book dispatches so finally. The vice is marginal, and the bibliography has its own fascination. *The Masters and the Slaves,* and the other two books of Gilberto's trilogy on the making of Brazil, *The Mansions and the Shanties* and *Order and Progress,* and all the satellite works like the book on sugar and confectionery, are in the end a single great Brazilian buildungsroman about the making of Gilberto, a Proustian attempt to recover his own past disguised as the description of a civilization.

II

A Cordial Man

Brazilians are Mediterranean and African in most of their ways
and as Mediterraneans they are lunch people. Big lunch people.
It is a problem in northeastern Brazil not to be a lunch person
and sometime after sundown that difficulty starts making itself
felt for a dinner person. People in Recife did their eating in the
day and their drinking in the evening. You could get a cheap
and abundant worker's lunch almost anywhere. And in a place
with white tablecloths and good china and uniformed waiters
bearing elaborate menus, you could get the kind of vast and
traditional midday meal described by Gilberto Freyre, consisting
of many dishes and side dishes served with spoon and fork,
expertly wielded by a single hand in the best French manner
against a background of *azulejos*—the beautiful blue-painted
white Portuguese tiles—dark wood, white linen and with whatever drink you fancied. At night all the enticing restaurants were
boarded up. Places where people drank did food of a kind, but
since food was an odd thing to look for in the evening they
weren't geared up to supply anything decent. This was where
the boys with broomsticks and braziers came in.

One evening I headed down a short narrow alley off one of

the busiest streets—the sun long down by now—and entered a calm cobbled space that was closed to traffic. A tall baroque church in eggshell blue with sandstone quoining rose behind a spiked railing at one end of the square. Narrow roads went off each corner, and the other three sides were lined by little colonial houses of one or two stories. The houses were painted in pastel colors, their ornaments picked out in white. Some of the houses had tables and chairs outside. People were drinking and the broomsticks and braziers were busy. People were even having their shoes shined.

None of the places had visible names, and the outside tables of one were continuous with the outside tables of the next. It was a beady eyed waiter who swept me in as I peered through the door. Even in the tropics I like to sit inside to eat or drink, to have a roof over my head and a solid wall behind me, a table that sits foursquare and a noncollapsible chair. Outside is edgy. So while the people outside, who were mostly young, were jostling over their drinks and prey to birds, mendicants, sudden rain, violent assault, unsteady tables and the importunities of tiny children and the entrepreneurial youth, I was waved into a room that was pleasingly half full. It had walls of white-painted brick, a dark wooden floor and a long communal table of heavy dark wood down the middle of the room, with long wooden benches to sit on. At the front, by the windows, and along the sides were smaller tables and stools.

At the back of the room, framed by a massive, irregularly shaped contraption of huge dark wood, was a low bar. Bent over a glass and grinding with a wooden pestle was a slightly built man of middle age with a beaky nose, sharp black eyes and spiky, ruffled iron gray hair. He wore a neat short-sleeved shirt and a severe pair of half-moon glasses sat low on his nose, loops of granny chain swinging on either side as he mashed a lime with sugar and ice to make a *caipirinha*. Behind him a massive old dresser's endless compartments held spirit bottles, postcards, openers, spike files of bills and receipts, photographs, a calendar, glasses of various sizes, several bunches of keys, pencils and a ballpoint pen, some paper flowers in a little vase, a bottle of some strange and murky homemade liqueur, a paperweight and a couple of little human figures in unglazed terracotta. On the dresser's main ledge was an ancient manual adding machine by Burroughs with a crank handle and a ribbon of white paper spilling out the back. To the left of the bar a stockade of varnished saplings led out to reeking pissoirs, and against the wall on the right was a further empty space, a little frame within the frame of the bar that from time to time was abruptly filled by a primitive dumbwaiter, hauled up on pulleys with a load of dirty glasses or lowered with a bump announcing plates of food. Behind the dresser a kind of stepladder led up through a square hole cut in the ceiling to a kitchen hidden under the eaves. From time to time a pair of well shaped and tanned bare female legs descended through the hole and rested on a rung, while their owner spoke with the beaky man behind the bar. The legs then rose again out of sight.

The waiters raced in and out with trays of sweating beer bottles and glasses wrapped in napkins. Sometimes they carried food, of which I tried to snatch a glimpse. The beer, which in Rio had always been draft, in Recife was always in bottles, and the bottles here were tended and nurtured in the freezer so that they emerged at zero degrees centigrade without having actually frozen, and arrived before you with a bluish frost on the glass like the bloom on a plum. From time to time there was a miscalculation, and the beer solidified when the crown cap was removed, spilling endless frozen amber foam like ice cream. Sometimes a customer would wander off without having paid and a waiter sprinted after him.

The man with the beaky nose worked away behind the fronds

of green coconuts, which were spilling out of a trough in the wooden contraption in front of the bar, grinding limes and ice into tumblers and adding the sugar and the slug of *cachaça* and presenting the drink with a white paper napkin folded around the base of the glass to absorb the condensation. Even when the trade winds moved the air after sunset, there was always condensation on the drinks glasses. Cachaça and beer were the universal drinks in Brazil. The beer was pale, cold, low in alcohol and superfluous sugars and malts and gases, and practically indistinguishable from one brand to another. At this time, however, in Recife the Antártica was being brewed with water from a mineral spring that made it ambrosial. Cachaça gave you a hit of something altogether more interesting. The white distillation of the sugarcane was not a fancy booze. Neat cachaça put fire in your belly and stilled the pangs of hunger. Caipirinhas gave you a simultaneous hit of ice's cold, alcohol's fire, lime's ascorbic acid and cane sugar's energy rush. In Recife the cachaça was Pitù, poured from the bottle with the picture of the red freshwater crustacean on the label. The same picture was on walls all over the city. The coconuts were there to have their ends hacked off with a murderous cleaver when someone wanted a glass of their juice. There were people drinking whiskey with coconut juice too. Juice extraction was deft and rapid. One hand wielded the cleaver, the other held the fruit for slicing and upended it over a waiting jug in a single movement while the other hand was replacing the cleaver on the bar. The cleaver was a worry, lying there on the bar, as things got lively.

Bangüê was the place's name. It was carved in big letters on a panel of varnished wood above the bar. I had stepped into the plantation world of Gilberto Freyre. A *bangüê* was several different things in slave life on the sugar plantations of early Brazil. Gilberto, describing *the morose, melancholy, indolent life* of the plantation wives in that man's world where the wives bore heirs and the men had slave women as their lovers, said they went out *only in the hammock . . . or in the bangüê, or litter,* with its leather top and curtains, carried by African slaves. A bangüê was also the stretcher that carried away the bodies of slaves when they died, and the hand barrow made out of liana thongs that was used to remove the used husks of the sugarcane. Bangüê became the name of the trough in which raw hides were washed and tanned. Bangüê—*one of the most characteristic of Brazilian regional terms, with a number of meanings and shades of meaning,* chipped in the translator in one of his footnotes—was also the furnace and the boiling pans in which the sugarcane juice was rendered down, or the tiled runnel in which it was drained off to crystallize and solidify, and so it got to be in the end the name given for the whole sugar producing estate in its collective sense, the plantation, the mill, the refinery, and now the drinking place that evoked this world.

The bar itself was a dark and massive wooden trough, with a great wooden beam horizontal above it and at one end a vertical wooden screw with its thread carved into a smoothed and polished tree trunk. The huge piece of wooden machinery must have come from one of Pernambuco's old sugar mills, like the old leg irons, balls and chains, and weapons of assault that hung on the walls. There was an ancient baby's crib made of reeds hanging from one wall of white-painted brick. There were a few knives and guns and some clay pipes for smoking. And there were a couple of big portrait photographs on the walls of sunbaked musicians from the drylands of the interior playing instruments they had made. There was also some rather fine wood carving on panels. On your way to the amenities you had to squeeze past a wooden sedan chair with round portholes for looking out the side, massive as the other plantation things, an unbelievable weight to stagger around with in the sun, even without one of the plantation wives—the women of the big house, who never lifted a finger on their own account, were seen with some malice in the sketches of European travelers—lapping over the sides in all her indolent melancholy. The sedan chair, minus the leather roof and curtains, was now being used to store beer crates in and was probably the eponymous bangüê itself. There were tottering stacks of beer crates, full and empty, by the door, and more between the shafts of the sedan chair. A thickset man in shorts, with twisted, powerful shoulders, came and went in a rapid oblique shuffle with crates on his back, changing empty bottles for full, staggering slightly under his load. A golden patina of old smoke covered the walls and nobody seemed to be there for the decor.

The hard-pressed waiter flung a menu down and it skidded across the polished wood. The list of the day was typed on a sheet of paper stapled to a woven reed fan, like a paddle with a handle, such as slave girls used to keep the air moving around their mistresses' necks and breasts as they swung in the hammock or the rocking chair. It was hard to choose. *Sarapatel. Arrumadinho. Chambaril. Xarque.* The waiter pursed his lips with concentration as I ordered a drink and then he shuffled off, a small sturdy workhorse in short-sleeved shirt and carpet slippers. The Bangüê had an excellent menu of a daily special for every day of the week except Sunday, but only for lunch. I was in trouble again. But only partly, and only for a while. The menu's longest section was its list of *petiscos,* and the place called itself a *petisqueira.* The petisco was a superior version of the snack. A simple snack in Brazil was a *lanche* and you found it in a *lanchonete,* or a glass box on wheels. A petisco, like a *quitute,* was altogether superior food, inventive, complex, refined, delicious— serious food for the serious drinker, to be shared around, had in any order or combination, wolfed down or picked at over time, and the Bangüê promised well. After flinging a couple of preliminary inquiries at the waiter, and getting rapid-fire answers that were too complex for a first go, I settled on *carne do sol com macaxeira.*

Sun dried steak might seem tough and overcooked, but it was always dense with flavor, enhanced by a few sautéed onion rings and complemented by the waxy translucency of boiled *macaxeira.* Macaxeira was a long pale root with a pinkish skin that might grow to a meter long, one of the kinds of manioc that were a Brazilian staple. Sellers wheeled stacks of them around the city in barrows, announcing themselves with a drawn out macaxeira street cry. The carne do sol arrived with a bottle of homemade *pimenta,* a suspension of pounded red chilies, and another bottle containing clarified butter. This was another product of the process that produced the white curd cheese, no less prized than the cheese itself and de rigueur with carne do sol. The next evening I had *agulhas fritas,* half a dozen fried needlefish neatly aligned along an oval plate. If you took the head and the tail in your fingers, the dry white flesh lifted neatly in a single piece on either side of the skeleton.

At what point, during what lull, did the bird of prey behind the bar acknowledge my presence? I no longer recall. The waiter, whose name was José Antônio, kept the cold beer arriving at the right moment, as each night I worked down the list of petiscos. One quiet moment early in the week the person behind the bar with the hooded eyes came over and we had a conversation about food. He talked as he looked, in such a rapid staccato way that a lot of his recommendations were lost, apart from breadfruit. Then he asked if I was a researcher.

Gilberto Freyre had brought me to Recife—or rather Gilberto's books, the man himself having died at eighty-nine three years before—and since Gilberto had had an insatiable curiosity about everything that was really human in Brazilian history and life, human in the sense of appetites, desires, pleasures, vices and consolations and the ways these were realized, as against the country's myths, illusions, lies and rationalizations, a curiosity about the details that made up the real rather than about sustaining big pictures, I said yes, I was a researcher. The bird of prey, whose name was Vavá, accent on the second *va,* short for Florisvaldo, didn't press me for details. He had known a number of researchers from the exterior—the exterior being anywhere not inside Brazil—and I seemed to fit the pattern. Most of the Europeans who did research in Pernambuco were looking into poverty, homelessness, malnutrition, illiteracy, corruption, violence, human rights violations, child labor, life expectancy, health problems and things like that. Problems of underdevelopment, and this was not material for conversation over an evening drink and a petisco. Other researchers came to Pernambuco to look into popular culture, oral traditions, the rituals of Carnival, dance and music, and if I was one of these, well, there was plenty of time.

Vavá jumped up and went back to work, to meet and greet, being best friend of every paying customer who crossed his threshold, to mix drinks and keep things moving. Almost hidden behind the dresser, there was another head behind the bar, staring out from among the green coconuts through giant designer lenses. The head belonged to a seated woman who was cranking away intermittently at the Burroughs calculator. She had a headful of golden ringlets, each one defined as if carved in stone, and large eyes behind the enormous glasses. She was Dona Lia, Vavá's wife, and Dona Lia was the business part of the Bangüê.

Vavá and Lia—it would take me ten years to find this out— were in crisis. They had taken over the bar as an offshoot of their main activity, which was a small art gallery of work produced by painters and sculptors and wood-carvers and potters in the interior of Pernambuco. The art gallery was in another little house not quite next door to the bar, and the back of this house, or its front, opened as a shop front onto the busy avenue running behind one side of the Pátio de São Pedro. That shop was a bookshop, the Livraria de Cordel, and as its name announced it sold the little booklets with the words of the ballads sung by the wandering singers at the bus stop. Vavá had started with the bookshop, selling the cordel libretti and other books about Pernambuco and the Northeast, and then set up as a dealer in local art. He and Lia had taken over the Bangüê when it came up for sale several years later. Taking on the bar turned out to be a smart move.

———

One night I stood by a parked truck not far from the Bangüê and listened to a man called Lula speak. It was a turbid evening after a hot wet winter's day. Night had fallen suddenly and hid the inky clouds that were trailing low over the city roofs. The truck was parked in a shallow triangular plaza, alongside the high iron railing that defended a seventeenth-century convent. The convent chapel's white baroque façade, edged in dark unpainted stone, glowed in the dark at the end of an avenue of palms. Behind the truck and next to the convent were the plain but blotchy dark green front and the dim fluorescent lights of the Parrot Restaurant, which at that hour was nearly empty of drinkers. Lula was a stocky, vigorous man with matted and kinky black hair growing low on his brow and a thick black beard on his face. He stood on the back of the truck in a worn short-sleeved shirt, leaning forward on one strong hairy forearm, looking down at the crowd of us standing around, and holding a microphone on the end of a cord. You could see he was missing a finger of the hand holding the microphone. Lula was a man like many in Recife. He might have come in from up-country Pernambuco to sell farm produce or buy stuff at the city's São José markets. Lula was a Brazilian battler, recognizably one of those northeastern battlers who hurled their stocky bodies into the daily struggle to put food on the table, and sometimes, like Lula, were taken a long way from home by the requirements of that struggle. There seemed to be a great intimacy in his words to the crowd. He wasn't raising his voice, and he wasn't making promises. He certainly wasn't spinning through any rhetorical hoops. He was just talking in a low-key, concrete, practical but utterly compelling way about the troubles in their lives and what, practically, could be done about these troubles.

Lula was more widely acquainted with the hardnesses of life than most of his listeners in Recife. He knew the underside of the industrial megalopolis down in the south of Brazil. Lula had been taken to São Paulo as a child, one of the millions of north-easterners who had made Brazil's great internal migration from drought and starvation to feed the industrial growth of the south. He had known, shining shoes and selling peanuts on the streets as a child, what it was to be despised as a northeasterner by big city people. After a remarkable few years as a union leader of São Paulo's metalworkers he had seen out the dictators and he was now a leader of the Workers' Party, that heterogeneous cluster of revolutionary Marxists, liberation theologians, ordinary parliamentary social democrats and trade unionists which had been formed ten years earlier, as the power of the military waned, to act for people whose voices had not been heard in Brazil for a long time. Lula himself was not an ideologue, or even much of a book reader. He had become the voice of the Workers' Party around Brazil for the same reason he had been so effective as the metalworkers' leader, for the same reason that I and dozens of others were now standing rapt in the dark as he spoke from a truck.

Listening to him speak, you forgot that a few months earlier, at the end of 1989, Lula had come remarkably close to being the president of Brazil and that he bore the mark of a loser.

Lula's recent nearness to power seemed an illusion, because the man who defeated Lula, when the two of them had pulled away from the other pretenders and gone to a final vote six months before, was now so compellingly Brazil's new leader that it was hard to imagine the vote could have gone otherwise. Fernando Collor de Mello was a northeasterner too, though he seemed to come from another world. You also forgot, looking at the dynamic new president, that a year earlier Fernando Collor and not Lula had seemed the unlikely candidate. Nobody knew much about Fernando. There didn't seem much to know. But he was tall, much taller than Lula, stylish in a way Lula could never be, apparently much younger, though the difference was four years, and very personable. He promised to modernize Brazil, after the decades lost by the military dictators, sell off the sclerotic state corporations, end protection, stop inflation, open up the economy and make Brazil globally competitive. This was advanced talk at the end of the 1980s, and it sounded fresher and more exciting in Brazil than anywhere. Fernando had a terrific TV presence—people were entranced by the jogging, the motorbikes, the glamour. They knew the lifestyle from TV. Fernando was the future.

Before the long night of the military, only a tiny group of Brazilians had ever been allowed to vote and the chosen one was always the choice of the landed wealthy, of the sugar people, the cattle people, the rubber people, the coffee people. Even so, in sixty years the country had elected only four presidents, and only two had seen out their terms. In 1954 Getúlio Vargas—*I am standing in a sea of mud*—retired to the presidential bedroom and put a bullet through his heart. Juscelino Kubitschek, who got Brasilia built in 1960, finished his term and handed over to an elected successor, but Juscelino himself was a creature of the military. In 1960 only one adult Brazilian in four was allowed to vote, and Jânio Quadros, who won, gave up after seven months as president, claiming *hidden forces* were forcing him out. His vice president, João Goulart, took over and was removed by the tanks and troops in 1964.

In 1985 the retreating military had let only the Congress vote for the president; the winner died and the first president of a newly democratic Brazil was little José Sarney, a northeastern landowner rooted in the past whom nobody had ever imagined as its leader. Brazil had changed out of sight since the military coup. It was now a complex industrial and metropolitan society and the vote of 1989 was momentous because it was the first really democratic election ever held in a country of 150 million people. It was momentous too because one of the candidates came from Brazil's industrial workforce, who made the country go and had no say in its running, and received the thinnest trickle of the immense wealth Brazil generated. Lula's presence was deeply disturbing to the players of the old game. After years of repression and then the bitter disappointment of 1985, a lot of Brazilians were feeling ready in 1989 to choose the man who wanted to change the rules entirely. The old players had no credit at all. Panic grew on the upper floors of São Paulo and in the mansions of Rio. Who could be found to represent big money and make big money's interests attractive to all those Brazilians who were struggling in the middle, eager to move up, afraid of being dragged down?

This was Fernando's chance. Up he popped, from a little state people had barely heard of, confident, articulate, visually strong, seemingly untied to the past and savage in his attacks on the outgoing president. The contest of 1989 was big enough and polarized enough to seize the imaginations of people outside Brazil, and the world watched from afar the relentless rise of the former metalworker and the drama of the charismatic unknown who looked like a playboy. In Italy I remembered the violence and decay of years before and suddenly I wished I could see what was happening in Brazil. People were turning out in hundreds of thousands to hear Lula in Rio and São Paulo in the days before the vote. Others were scared of Lula's radical words and soothed by Fernando's talk of modernizing Brazil, and saw Fernando as a hope for change without pain. How could you tell, unless you were there? By the time I got to Brazil it was all over, and Fernando had been sworn in a couple of months earlier and here was Lula on the stump for some local man. But I hadn't lost my curiosity. This was my research. I had no idea then how much these lives might show about the oddest and most thrilling country in the Western Hemisphere.

It started raining again while Lula spoke, lightly at first, then heavier and heavier. The sound of the water falling on the stones almost drowned the noise of Lula's amplified words coming from the clusters of loudspeakers. Umbrellas were useless under the weight of the water. Office workers who had stopped to listen held plastic satchels over their heads. It was all useless. Shirts were plastered to shoulders and hair was flattened on scalps. Shoes filled with water. Beads of rain were caught by the spotlights as they gathered in heavy pearls along the ropes of electric cable that looped from overhead lines to the truck and the speakers and the lights and snaked along the ground and through pools of water. What if the cables came down? Lula went on talking calmly, his four fingers gripping the mike, standing upright and beating the rain with his other arm now for emphasis. Nobody moved until he finished.

The rain was still falling heavily when the loudspeakers played a hymnlike little tune sung by quavering maudlin voices. It was called "Our Star Is Going to Shine." This was the new anthem of the Workers' Party. The star was the red star of revolutionary class struggle, but some in the party had decided that the color and the imagery and the talk that went with them were putting people off, people who might otherwise be won over, like housewives and others unlikely to clench a fist. A few less people frightened and Lula might be changing the world in Brasilia, instead of standing on the back of a truck in the rain. The jingle was one of the direst inventions of the newer and nonthreatening Workers' Party that was quietly being elected to the government of more and more cities and states around Brazil. The jingle sounded like something heard in one of the evangelical sect halls that dotted Brazil ever more thickly. The new and militantly evangelical churches, some of them huge and vastly rich already, were deeply hostile to the Workers' Party. The hostility was reciprocated. Evangelists were the other contenders for the hearts and minds of the Brazilian masses. It was no mistake that the Workers' Party's sickening new song sounded like an evangelical hymn. From the music or the rain, the crowd scattered fast and headed for shelter as soon as Lula finished speaking.

The odd darting figure, satchel still gripped over head, was still running for cover. Otherwise the streets themselves were empty now. Along their edges in the shadows were the night people, black on black, gripping their flattened cardboard boxes and their small children, huddled under available overhangs, waiting for the storm clouds to exhaust themselves so they could go to bed. A few older children stalked apart like wingless insects, emaciated and detached from the human clusters, gray rags flapping off their limbs. Their heads were mostly shaved and they clutched glue bottles to their breastbones, under their filthy knotted T-shirts and running singlets. They looked serenely beyond all human care. The next day was blue on blue, gold on white, hot and dazzling.

Harried José the waiter was clearly one of the ground down northeastern working people Lula spoke for. José used to set off on his interminable journey home toward midnight, after hours and hours on his half-crippled feet. He worked only some days and received no salary. Like all the bar waiters he made only the ten percent service charge on the drinks he served and he lost the price of the drinks when a client absconded. This was why he looked harried, throwing anxious glances out the window every time he came inside to pick up a new order. He looked, as Vavá pointed out once with a seraphic detachment that contained a feeling he couldn't afford to indulge, many years older than his real age. One night I mentioned Lula. José's face grew twisted with dislike, and with a kind of embarrassment. Lula was ignorant, incompetent, illiterate. He hadn't been fit to lead Brazil. What would people think if he went overseas? Lula had done pretty well in the Northeast, and splendidly here in his own state of Pernambuco, but it suddenly became clear why he hadn't won Brazil. José hadn't wanted Lula as his president because Lula was too like himself. Slumming foreigners might look on Lula as a working class hero, but when José saw him he felt pained and humiliated and he hated himself and Brazil. He wanted to be represented not by a stumpy bearded metalworker who had lost a finger in a lathe and got lost in Portuguese syntax, but by a tall, elegantly suited and mellifluous graduate in law, a person who knew the world and could meet with foreign leaders as an equal and an ornament to Brazilian civilization. Someone like Fernando.

Fernando and Lula seemed to come from different countries, and in a sense they did. Brazil was a country where the richest one percent of the people had fifteen percent of the wealth. The poorest forty percent had less than a tenth. If you looked at the gap between the wealth of the richest twenty percent of Brazilians and what the poorest twenty percent had, Brazil came in at the bottom of a list of eighty-five countries. The gap between rich and poor was more than six times the difference in countries like India, Egypt, Pakistan, Indonesia. It was more than double the wealth gap in Russia, Mexico, Nigeria. Double the gap in Chile, Venezuela, Colombia too—the only Latin American country that came anywhere close to Brazil's inequalities was Guatemala. Brazil's wealth gap was more than six times Japan's or Germany's, four times Canada's, more than three times the differences in Britain, the United States or Australia. If you compared wealth inequalities in the countries of the world, Brazil came third to last in a list of the ninety-three countries for which data existed. Fernando was a winner in a country where Lula and all the people like him were born to lose. The Brazilian people themselves had just confirmed it.

Fernando's first act of modernization was a shock for almost everyone. The day after he took office in 1990, Brazilians woke to find the government had confiscated, for eighteen months, all their money in the bank, above a ceiling of just over a thousand dollars. People were not reassured when the new minister of the economy was unable to explain on TV just how the Collor Plan was going to stabilize the currency. One morning after breakfast, and a couple of months after the freeze, I met the hotel's owner in the lift. The lift took some time to come down from the terrace with its view and its breakfast spread, and as it descended the owner filled the space with praise of Fernando. He thought the shock to the system a great thing and told me Fernando was going to save Brazil. A few days later the Bangüê hiked its prices and so did everywhere else. Fernando's plan was already falling apart.

People who had saved now had no money to buy houses or cars, pay schools and hospitals, even to buy food. They certainly had no money to buy works of art. For years Vavá and Lia had been buying the work of artists in outback Pernambuco, mostly carved wood and ceramic figures, and selling it to galleries and collectors in Brasilia, São Paulo and Rio, selling it from their own gallery in the Pátio. Vavá loved being an art entrepreneur and suddenly it was over. He was left with a houseful of carvings and pottery, paintings and fabrics that would get dustier and dustier over the months and years. The Bangüê had become his only hope of making a living. It was why Lia so often paused as she cranked the calculator and stared into space. Things were quiet even in the bar, though business picked up as inflation ballooned again. Two months after bank accounts were frozen, inflation was running at eight percent a month. By November it would be seventeen percent a month. The faster prices rose, the busier the street dealing got and the fuller the bars. I never understood why.

There was one client of the Bangüê's who even in the slow times turned up every evening around six and stayed for an hour or so. He was the only person in the bar who ever wore a jacket and tie, usually a bone colored tropical linen jacket in patrician style. Among the dark wood and the country appurtenances he looked like the plantation owner. He was in his forties, had an amiable face and smiled often under a large dark mustache, and he had a bon vivant's girth. He never sat down, and drank whiskey standing up by the serving bar, wedged between the green coconuts and the stacks of plates and glasses, in front of the dumbwaiter. He stood by the bar so he could speak to Vavá, and the two of them carried on a lively conversation the whole time he was there, inches from the whirling cleaver splitting coconuts. From time to time Vavá would pass him a little plate of cheese with *pimenta* or something special that didn't seem to be on the menu. He never seemed to pay for anything, and I wondered about that.

His name was Cândido and we started talking one evening, over the noise and clatter of the food and drinks. Somehow, we got on to abandoned children. Cândido asked me how serious the street children problem was in Italy. *Street children?* I said. *We don't have any.* A wave of child thieves from the Balkans was

just then sweeping through the city streets of Italy—hardly
abandoned though. They were slaves run by gangs of adults who
tortured them at night if their takings fell short. Their number
was relatively tiny. In Italy proper even the street children of
Naples were gone. And even in the hardest times, these had
always had, if not a family, a locality, a context, a sustaining
social fabric they were part of. In Brazil, the street children
seemed to number in the millions, and they had no real ties to
the adult world at all. Recife teemed with skeletal child glue
sniffers. They were the bottom layer of a whole heap of Brazilian
children abandoned by the society they were born into, a society
whose violence in home and neighborhood made them take their
chance on the streets as the lesser evil. The glue didn't always
get the children through the day. You needed more than an
intoxicating sniff to defend yourself. There were no less desperate
adults also on the streets, and other adults who wanted to use
you, and other adults again who simply saw you as detritus,
something to be removed by whatever means were at hand. Four
street children were murdered every day in Brazil—probably
more, every day, every year. How were Cândido and I to talk
about this? His affability was subdued for a moment.

———

Brazil's new economics minister, who thought up the bank seizure and found it so hard to explain, was a young woman called
Zelia. She was a protégée of Fernando's from his tiny home state
of Alagoas in the Northeast. Zelia had no experience of politics
and little of economics, or of life. The day after bank accounts
were frozen, Zelia turned up unannounced at the president's
home in Brasilia. Two days in office, Fernando was not so intimidated by his new job that he didn't feel able to relax. Zelia
found him relaxing over a prelunch whiskey and deep in con-

versation with a middle-aged man—bald, thickset, his face lightly masked by big designer glasses and a mustache. The thickset man was drinking gin. *An admirer of British habits, at lunchtime he recommended a Tanqueray, his favorite, with a slice of lemon fixed on the edge of the glass.* As Fernando glared at Zelia over his tumbler of Black Label, angry at being disturbed, the bald man affably *raised his glass a little, combining the offer of a drink with friendly greeting.* Fernando said, *What are you doing here?*

Zelia knew the middle-aged man. He too was from the little state of Alagoas, whose capital, Maceió, was on the coast not far south of Recife. He had been Fernando's campaign treasurer, the man who paid for everything. He had paid her, when she was an unknown economist on Fernando's election team, thirty thousand dollars cash plus expenses for each of the last six months before the final vote. His name was Paulo César Cavalcanti de Farias and when the election was finally won Fernando had told him, *Without you I wouldn't even have made it to the second round,* but hardly anyone else knew of his role in Fernando's victory. For PC Farias, whose friends called him PC, this private praise from the president was enough. The people who did know PC were nearly all from Alagoas.

When Zelia interrupted them halfway through the president's second day in office, PC and Fernando were talking about a matter that had grown from the way PC had run Fernando's campaign finances the year before. PC had done too well. He had raked in $160 million and had only spent $100 million on getting Fernando elected. *What am I going to do with these sixty million dollars, Fernando?* PC had asked. PC had never seen so much money in his life, and was still a bit dazed by the liberality with which people had given. The election had been close, and people had responded generously, even extravagantly, to PC's solicitations. Several of Brazil's banks had given $3 or $4 million each, and all the big industrial groups had given at least as much. Andrade Gutierrez, the construction, telecommunications and real estate group, gave more than $7 million. Almost none of the people with money to lose had let PC down. The more they had to lose and the higher Lula rose in the opinion polls the more freely they had given. Only the Globo media group failed to give to PC.

Manage it, Fernando told PC of the $60 million. It was an unusually large amount of spare money to manage, but electing a president was an unusual experience for Brazil. Fernando was happy to have the money and didn't want to be bothered with details. PC saw it as a challenge. He had to manage letters of credit, stocks and shares, cash checks, bank checks, checks from account holders who didn't exist, bills of exchange, dollar notes, dollars held in offshore accounts. The gifts had come in all these forms and all the gifts were a long way outside the law's idea of the acceptable present. PC managed to manage the money and in the months after the election he paid out $2 million of it for Fernando's personal and family expenses. PC learned a lot from the big industrialists who had given the money—new ways of money laundering, new ways to keep money hidden inside Brazil and offshore, refinements in the methodology of keeping parallel accounts. He set up new offshore companies and opened bank accounts in the Caribbean, the United States, France and Switzerland. For the first few months of Fernando's presidency, he paid out in cash or in checks drawn on his own accounts. Later that year he worked out a system of payment by checks from nonexistent account holders and he stuck to this.

PC had been Fernando's treasurer for four years, ever since the campaign that saw Fernando elected governor of their home state of Alagoas. PC had smoothed away an impasse between Fernando and the sugar growers. He had always been more than a money man. He was Fernando's mediator with the business world and the administrator of Fernando's own affairs. Fernando, who was an impatient person, came to rely on PC almost entirely in money matters, to the point where it was unclear quite what money was whose. For his part, Fernando had the social and political connections that PC's business activities required. Quite early in the campaign, when all was still in doubt, PC had gambled $2 million of his own money—a lot for him in those days—held in a Panama bank, on Fernando's election. *I'm staking everything I've got on this,* he told his incredulous brother. Fernando's fortunes and PC's now rose together. The symbiosis was total. When Zelia asked the president what to do about PC's intrusions into her running of Brazil's economy, Fernando told her, *Play along.* And Zelia, who was minister of the Brazilian economy, did what she was told by PC, who was no one at all.

The commonality of goods meant there was something for PC in the surplus. He paid himself back the two million from his Panama account. He finished off the house he was building, a $5 million concrete fortress on a hilltop whose interior was done out with priceless baroque religious carvings, contemporary designer kitsch and things PC had picked up on his travels, and whose master bedroom suite took up fifty square meters. PC also spent $10.5 million on a couple of jet planes for himself. He loved flying and he loved planes and nursed a secret plan to own a major airline. In one of his planes he flew his biggest giver, Sergio Andrade, from Rio to Havana. The Andrade Gutierrez group was interested in building floating oil platforms for Cuba and PC himself wanted to do business with Havana. Fidel Castro took them to dinner and gave PC a box of cigars personalized with the name *Don Pablo* on the band of each. From then on PC received regular supplies of these from the Cuban embassy in Brasilia, and he liked to talk about these gifts from Fidel, who seemed to have understood from the start exactly what the game was.

One Friday afternoon I moved to a cheaper hotel. A run-down place in a dilapidated nineteenth-century mansion by the river looked dense with character, and so it was. On the verandah a very tall, very old and very thin black man rocked all day in his rocking chair with a flat checked cap tipped down over his eyes. The building stank of rancid fat and the hot shower device in the bathroom gave out nasty electric shocks when you turned on the water. Shortly before daybreak someone in the street below took out my windowpane with a rifle, filling the bed with glass shards. It seemed time to move on. From a classified advertisement in the *Diario de Pernambuco* I found a flat on one of the upper floors of a huge and scary block of low-rent housing. The building was so vast and its cardboard thin walls of crumbling cement so flimsy that it felt ready to fold up and collapse at any moment. The walls vibrated with the life they were so imperfectly built to contain and big pieces of the honeycomb brickwork enclosing the staircase that spiraled up the side of the building had already fallen off into space. The holes in the staircase wall, the torn patches of blinding light, induced vertigo. When the lifts didn't work you climbed thirteen floors past these sudden holes. The lifts when they did work were so few and so slow and their users so many that you could make that climb in the time you waited for a packed and sweaty ride.

At dawn on Saturday I woke to a tremendous banging on the door. I jumped out of bed into ankle deep water. The next door neighbor was banging to warn me. He was a black schoolteacher who said people on the floor above had gone away for the weekend leaving a tap on and a sink plugged. *They're always doing this,* he yelled over the sound of cascading water at the end of the passage. He told me that the entire building went without water during the daylight hours—unpaid bills, the teacher said.

People had to collect their daily needs during the night. Our neighbors had left town with the tap turned on while the water was cut off. Their apartment was locked and nobody had a key. I noticed now that all the front doors on this floor except mine were protected by a flood barrier across the floor. I spent the rest of the morning trying to sweep water out of the flat, along the corridor and down the stairs, encouraged by a neighbor, whose light dress was tucked well up around her thighs on account of the ankle deep water. Then the building's water was cut off again.

Dried out, the apartment was basic and practically unfurnished. I learned to shower after dark and before dawn. The window had a splendid outlook on the city and the sea. And if you looked straight down there was a wide ledge below, not much above street level, and beyond the ledge a narrow pedestrian alley which ran the length of the block and was filled with the tiny stalls of locksmiths, cobblers, knife sharpeners and the folding tin tables and chairs of a string of tiny bars which interspersed the shops, each of which had its own improvised awning of translucent corrugated plastic. The people in the building used to throw their rubbish, quite big bags of it at times, out of their windows. Most of it landed on the ledge and slowly disintegrated there in the sun and the rain. Pleasure in the view was always punctuated by a falling plastic bottle or a floating ice cream carton, and it was unwise to put your head outside. Sometimes a bag of kitchen scraps tossed distractedly from an upper floor would miss both the ledge and the awnings and land from a great height on a group of citizens relaxing over a cold beer. From above it looked as though an ants' nest had been poked with a stick. Inside the building, my neighbor the teacher had an endlessly active social life and his rambunctious visitors—his students? surely not—were soon mistaking my door for his and banging at two in the morning. There was a great deal of coming and going at all hours of day and night in the Edifício Ipiranga. And just over the road was the bus stop for the beach.

The beach at Boa Viagem was a long, long narrow strip of sand that ran north-south behind an exiguous rib of rock a few meters out from the shore. Boa Viagem was the new part of town, the usual strip development, blocks of apartments built along the beachfront and a promenading pavement of mosaic stones in the Rio manner, with coconut juice stalls at intervals. Farther back were the hypermarkets, the shopping malls and barbecue joints as big as football grounds. At high tide the reef was covered, and at low tide in many places there was no water at all between sand and rock. In other places, and when the tide was halfway, shallow warm protected pools formed where the slothful wallowed for hours and small children played and peed. I always struck out well beyond the reef, looking for clearer water away from the crowds and wanting to get some distance covered. I never did find really clear water. *The abattoir outlet,* Vavá explained.

III

On the Beach

———————————

Black winter squalls would roll up over Recife, blowing sheets of rain off the Atlantic. Winter on the northeast seaboard was never cool though often wet and stormy. Fine days were for swimming and on the beach you needed a drink supplier and deck chair provider, who kept an eye on your things while you were in the water. I settled with Neuza because she was the only woman, a single mother competing with a congeries of inter-related family groups strung along the sand. Neuza was a lean and rangy black woman who might have been an athlete. She had three teeth left in her head and three small sons by three absconding fathers, the eldest eleven and the youngest barely able to walk.

Neuza did all the work. Her elder sons, who had long thin limbs like her though they were much lighter skinned, were too dreamy and distrait and far too weak to help their mother move the heavy blue wooden cart across the soft sand. The cart held the tub with ice and bottles, and the folded chairs and umbrellas when it was time to go.

Sometimes a squall swept in out of a brilliant morning. Black clouds and driving rain came up from nowhere over the sea, and the rain was so cold on the skin that people ran for the shelter of coconut palms or huddled under the umbrellas. One mean day, bad enough to keep almost everyone off the beach, Neuza saw from some way off a gang of marauding youths moving down the beach. We tucked such valuables as we had under the struts of the umbrella and gathered the chairs in a defensive circle around the cart. The wind howled off the ocean as the menacing long limbed figures got nearer, strung out along the beach, looking for trouble, and raised flying sand around their feet. The kids watched them silently. There was nothing we could do if they attacked us. Neuza's eyes were narrowed and wary. She had recognized these boys from a long way off and knew the signals. We can't have looked worth the trouble and so they passed us by, heading south, shorts and T-shirts flapping in the wind, wild and scary in that moment as the sky.

Whatever the weather a long train of food vendors trudged along the sand in an interminable caravan. The ones of most interest bore boiled prawns and fresh oysters—they were the ones you saw at the Pátio in the evening if a downpour had interrupted beach sales. One lady who always sold out early wore a kerchief and aluminum framed glasses and left the island of Itamaracá—an island of the delta with a big Dutch fort from the seventeenth century—before dawn to get to the beach with a fat lidded aluminum cooking pot on her head. In the pot were big red and white shelled mud crabs from the island, caught by her husband and boiled in the pot with coconut milk, palm oil and unidentifiable African spices. The oysters were also from Itamaracá and when they arrived I forgot the cholera lately come from Peru and sweeping northern Brazil. A boy knelt in the sand by his galvanized bucket, levering open shell after shell with a broken bladed knife. On each a single drop of fresh lime juice was enough, and gulps of Neuza's cold Antártica.

If you kept on going south along this beach, and followed the coast for twelve or thirteen hundred kilometers—until you were halfway to Rio or just past that point—you got to the place where the Portuguese first landed on this continent. Pedro Álvares Cabral was supposed to be heading around Africa to India in 1500 when he happened on the coast of Brazil. It seemed an odd mistake to make. The Portuguese navigators were consummate realists, empirical and incremental and quite unlike brilliant, mad Columbus, who had landed in the Caribbean eight years earlier, trying to sail westward to Asia and believing he had got there. The Portuguese were not people to sail off into the unknown. They had turned down Columbus's proposal of a westward sailing exploration because they already had a lot invested in getting to Asia by sailing east around Africa. Since 1433 Portuguese ships had been sailing farther and farther down the African coast, ready to strike east. One of their ships had already reached the mouth of the Congo by 1484, and four years later Bartolomeu Dias rounded the cape at the bottom of the continent. Only a mutiny made him turn back.

Then Vasco da Gama made the full sea journey around Africa to Asia. He reached Calicut, the great pepper emporium on the Malabar coast of India and was back in Lisbon in the summer of 1499. Portugal, one of the smallest and poorest countries in Europe, with a population of little more than a million, was now preparing to set up a string of fortified trading stations along East Africa and the coast of India, as it had already done along the Atlantic coast of Africa. The follow-up expedition left Lisbon the next spring. Pedro Álvares Cabral commanded thirteen ships carrying twelve hundred men, the most formidable Atlantic fleet ever assembled, and ready for the longest sea voyage ever made. They sailed out of the Tagus in March 1500. The ships took supplies for an eighteen-month voyage and cargo for the Portuguese trade offensive in Asia. The northeast trade winds carried Cabral's fleet past the Canary Islands in five days and down the coast of Africa. A week later they passed the Cape Verde Islands. Then one of the ships disappeared in the night, apparently in calm weather, and was never seen again. The other twelve ships spent two days searching for it, and perhaps lost their bearings. In any case, the fleet sailed far to the west of any expected course down Africa. After six weeks at sea and four weeks after passing the Cape Verde Islands, the sailors saw great quantities of drifting seaweed, and the next morning they saw shearwaters flying above their ships. That evening they caught sight of land, a high round mountain dominating a strip of coast. It was the unknown and still unnamed Brazil. They called it the Land of the True Cross, a name which would fail to stick, and they called the mountain Monte Pascoal because it was Easter.

The fleet anchored offshore and next morning they made out seven or eight people on the beach by a river mouth. By the time the Portuguese landed a boat there were eighteen or twenty Tupi waiting to greet them. The first meeting of Europe and South America was very friendly. The sleek and naked locals seemed quite unfazed by the sudden arrival of smelly bearded white people wearing clothes.

> They were dark and quite naked, with nothing to cover their shame. They carried bows in their hands with their arrows. They all came boldly toward the boat, and Nicolo Coelho made a sign to them to lay down their bows, and they laid them down. He couldn't converse with them, or reach any useful understanding, because of the surf breaking on the shore.

In return for a couple of sailors' caps, the leader of the landing party got *a hat of long bird feathers with a little tuft of red and grey feathers like a parrot's . . . a large string of very small white beads like seed pearls.* The next day *two well built natives* were removed from their canoe and as evening fell were brought on board Cabral's flagship, *where they were received with much pleasure and festivity.* It was a chance to get a good look at these unknown men from the unknown land. The Portuguese were struck by the *well shaped* people with *good faces and good noses,* and most of all that *they go naked, without any covering; neither do they pay any more attention to concealing or exposing their shame than they do to showing their faces, and in this respect they are very innocent.*

The locals were also unnervingly unimpressed by the display of European wealth and rank that Cabral put on. Only one of them caught sight of Cabral's gold neck chain *and began to point with his hand toward the land, as though he were telling us that there were gold in the land.* There was doubtless a general narrowing of eyes on the Portuguese side at this point in the meeting of the cultures. When the visitors lay down to sleep on board, attention returned to their nudity.

> . . . they stretched out on their backs on the carpet to sleep without taking any care to cover their privy parts, which were not circumcized, and the hair on them was well shaved and arranged.

The men he saw on the beach later were the same. *None of them was circumcized, and all were as we were.* No trace of Islamic contamination in the land of the true cross. If the members of the Portugese fleet felt a little abashed at the *innocent* and insolent physical well-being of the smooth skinned and glossy haired Tupi warriors they encountered, the sensation sharpened into something more when they met the Tupi girls. When Pero Vaz de Caminha was deputed to write an account of this landfall for the Portuguese king, the detached tone faltered when he described the young women. This wasn't like telling your king about an unusual headpiece of yellow tropical feathers, or a bone-pierced lower lip.

> There were three or four young girls among them, very young and very pretty, with very dark hair, long over their shoulders, and their privy parts so high, so closed and so free from hair that we felt no shame in looking at them very well . . . One of the girls was all painted from head to foot . . . and she was so well built and so rounded and her lack of shame was so charming that many women of our land, seeing such attractions, would be ashamed that theirs were not like hers.

The words were perhaps interpolated precisely to arouse the interest of Dom João II in the new land. Cabral sent his men ashore to check out the river and on its bank, Pero Vaz de Caminha told his king, they found

> four or five young women just as naked, who were not displeasing to the eye, among whom was one with her thigh from the knee to the hip and buttock all painted with that black paint and all the rest in her own colour; another had both knees and calves and ankles so painted, and her privy parts so nude and exposed with such innocence that there was no shame. There was another young woman carrying an infant boy or girl tied to her breasts by a cloth of some sort so that only its little legs showed. But the legs of the mother and the rest of her were not concealed by any cloth.

The beauty of the surroundings and the climate, the abundance of food and fresh water, and the untroubled relations with the extremely beautiful local people seemed, as much as the sheer glorious unexpectedness of this landfall, to create a little pocket of pleasure and refreshment out of time for Cabral's thousand or so men. Ahead lay the South Atlantic crossing, Africa, the Cape of Storms, the Indian Ocean, African tribesmen, Arab traders and Asian potentates, riot, massacre and death by water far from home. Many of those who came ashore on this Brazilian beach would never live to complete the journey home to Lisbon. One of their ships had vanished already, in calm weather and known latitudes. The landing turned into a picnic. Diogo Dias, one of the Portuguese captains—and brother of the Bartolomeu Dias who had rounded the African cape twelve years earlier—

> an agreeable and pleasure loving man . . . began to dance among them, taking them by the hands, and they were all delighted and laughed and accompanied him very well to the sound of the pipe . . . making many light turns and a remarkable leap which astonished them, and they laughed and enjoyed themselves greatly.

This palled eventually, and the Tupi got bored with the capering of Diogo Dias. Caminha reported more critically of their lack of appreciation that *they soon became sullen like wild men and went away upstream.* The sourness passed after a few days of familiarity and growing trust. Delight kept breaking down the walls of Caminha's own reserve, his sense of belonging to a superior culture, as he wrote to his king. The Portuguese were entirely dependent on the Tupi for fresh water and peace of mind, and the Tupi *skipped and danced with us to the sound of one of our tambours, in such a manner that they are much more our friends than we theirs.* While the Portuguese celebrated mass on an island in the bay the locals pleased them by following attentively, until interest sagged during the sermon. Many of the Tupi, knowing a celebration when they saw one, *got up and blew a horn or trumpet and began to leap and dance for a while.* When the ships' carpenters made a large wooden cross the Tupi were far more gripped by their encounter with the new technology than with the symbol of the true religion. In this enthralling moment they discovered the cutting power of metal tools, and pressed in *more to see the iron tools with which they were making it than to see the cross, because they have nothing of iron . . . they cut their wood and boards with stones.*

At the next mass the visitors were so pleased by the way the locals imitated their acts of worship that it seemed *these people to be wholly Christian lack nothing except to understand us.* One young woman who stayed throughout the mass was intent on following the ritual, but her total nudity distracted the Portuguese men from their prayers. They gave her a blanket, but *she did not think to spread it much to cover herself . . . The innocence of this people is such that that of Adam could not have been greater.* The new arrivals couldn't take their eyes off the bodies of the people they found. At first Caminha presented them as wild creatures, easily frightened, *rather like birds or wild animals . . . and their bodies are so clean, and so sleek and beautiful.* Invidious comparisons and a little abashed self-awareness inevitably followed. The Portuguese couldn't help linking the locals' physical beauty and their good natures. *Our Lord gave them fine bodies and good faces as to good men.* Like the lilies of the field,

> they do not till the soil or breed stock, nor is there ox or cow or goat or sheep or hen, or any other domestic animal which is used to living with men. Nor do they eat anything except these manioc . . . and the seeds and the fruits which the earth and trees produce. Yet they are stronger and better fed than we are with all the wheat and vegetables we eat.

Maybe the Portuguese weren't so superior after all. Could they really consider themselves healthier or happier? In Caminha's letter to the king his honesty went beyond the sharpness and accuracy and abundance of his reporting—and all his detail was ethnographically exact—and admitted a deep personal uncertainty into the larger and increasing wonder of the meeting with these people. As his letter went on, the rhetoric of the sales pitch gave way to an unfeigned sense of wonder.

The message was significant enough and urgent enough for a ship to be detached from the fleet to take it home to Lisbon. It touched carefully on the matters of interest to an empire building Christian king, on the theological—the unsullied souls ripe for conversion—and the commercial—the benign climate, abundant flora and fauna, signs of mineral resources. Yet in the very meticulousness of his recording of what the Portuguese found in the new land, and even more as he described the realities of their encounter with its people, Caminha kept sounding like a delighted boy writing home about the holiday of a lifetime. There was the beauty and animation of the people. There were also the birds, the *very large and beautiful red parrots,* macaws the sailors got for trinkets, *and two little green ones.* The Portuguese also got some green feather caps by barter, *and a cloth of feathers of many colours, woven in a very beautiful fashion.* And fish, signs of cockles and mussels, shrimps, *a very large and fat shrimp such as I had never seen before.*

There is no record of what the Tupi thought as their weird looking visitors sailed out onto the ocean, leaving behind two weeping convicts to be consoled. The convicts were guinea pigs, saved from death sentences back home, brought to be abandoned, to *learn their language well and understand them* and maybe even impart a little Christianity. Mainly the convicts were breeding stock. With a population a fifteenth the size of France's, a seventh Spain's, a third even of little England's, the only way tiny Portugal was going to people its new overseas territories was by engendering colonists in situ with the help of the locals. Nobody knows what thoughts of relief, regret or puzzlement passed through the minds of the Tupi and entered their conversation. Did they have any notion the Portuguese would be back? These particular Portuguese would not return. Within a few months Pero Vaz de Caminha, the author of one of the most tough minded and enchanting letters in the history of Europe, the sole document of a moment of perfect poise in the history of the Old World and the New, would be dead. He was killed in a fight with the people of Calicut on the Indian coast. Cabral himself, who was only thirty when he was given command of the intercontinental expedition, made it back to Lisbon the following year. But once home he behaved badly, fell out of favor with the king and died in obscurity.

The visitors' interest in the unmodified state of the Tupi penis expressed more than mere curiosity. The Portuguese knew a lot about Islamic culture. Portugal itself had been ruled by Islamic powers for five hundred years. Business and religion were inextricably interwined and the Portuguese were increasingly in competition with Arab traders. In 1415 the Portuguese had taken Ceuta, the outpost at the entrance to the Mediterranean on the tip of Morocco. Having gained a foothold in Africa they were setting out to break the Arab monopoly on the spice trade east of Africa and at the same time take the place Venice had long held as Europe's trade link with Asia. The Portuguese knew how rich Venice had become in the eastern Mediterranean by exploiting Asia's overland routes. The trade route through the Persian Gulf was closed to the Venetians after the Turks took Constantinople in 1453, and the Red Sea route was monopolized by Egyptian and Arabian traders. By pioneering a sea route from Europe around Africa to Asia, the Portuguese were about to displace both Arabs and Venetians and change the pattern of world trade forever. By landing in South America on the way, the Portuguese would project Europe irrevocably toward the west. A year and a half later the Florentine banker and cosmographer Amerigo Vespucci sailed into a vast and splendid bay a little farther north of Cabral's landing place, and called it the Bay of All Saints after the day of his arrival, which in Portuguese was the *Bahia de Todos os Santos*. Vespucci, who now went on as far south as Patagonia, had sailed along the northern coast of South America in 1499, and unlike Columbus he understood that this continent had no precedent in European thinking. He wrote home to Lorenzo de' Medici that a *new world* had been found.

Two months later the Portuguese Gonçalo Coelho sailed into another huge and no less splendid bay to the south, gorgeously jungled and marked out by monolithic rocks as big as mountains. The Tupi who lived there called it Guanabara. It looked to Coelho like the mouth of a great river, though it wasn't, and since it was New Year's Day of 1502 he called the place of his landfall the *Rio de Janeiro*. There were more expeditions over the next few years, and then in 1530 Portugal sent out four hundred men to set up a colony on the continent. It was the beginning of Brazil. In the early sixteenth century Cabral's meeting with the Tupi, and the other encounters that soon followed, revived the dream of a lost human innocence and the nostalgic longing for a golden age, just as the mental skies of Europe darkened and the continent's societies were riven by religious reformation and counterreformation. For all the hunter-gatherer tribes of Tupi and Guarani and the others who lived strung along the entire eastern littoral of the South American continent, their gifts of beautiful feathers, fresh water and sexual relief, and their discovery of metal technology and the taste of alcohol, were the beginning of the end.

Cabral's version of events, the magical accident set out in Pero Vaz de Caminha's letter, is in some ways hard to swallow. The founding document of Brazil's history may be more disingenuous than it seems, and Cabral's landfall less fortuitous. There is something odd, for a start, in the way the convoy should somehow have lost its bearings so badly that it drifted right across the Atlantic without the commanders' even realizing where they were until the ships made landfall in South America. This was a formidably equipped fleet, manned by the best seamen and navigators there were, using the best existing maps and the new Portuguese technology of the astrolabe to find its bearings astronomically, advancing in good weather down the well-known part of the African coast on its way to India, along the sea route pioneered by the Portuguese themselves. The letter doesn't ask whether the Land of the True Cross is just another island or part of something larger, as if Cabral and his king already had a very good idea what it was. There is a certain lack of *surprise* in the letter at the fact of the portentous landfall itself, and once the visit was over, the ships' commanders seemed again to know exactly where they were. Things resumed with their usual efficiency, one ship peeling off and heading directly home to Lisbon with the letter for Dom João while the rest of the convoy resumed its journey to India, having claimed the territory for Portugal and lost barely a week making the reconnoiter of the coast.

Given the expertise and daring of Portuguese seamen, and the state-of-the-art design of their oceangoing caravels, and the Portuguese government's determination to develop a maritime trading network ahead of its European rivals—Spain above all—there may have been earlier and unpublicized, not to say highly secret, Portuguese explorations across the Atlantic, following or even preceding Columbus's Caribbean discoveries. The race for the west in the 1490s was seen as a question of survival, and the competition between Spain and Portugal was so tense that the pope intervened in the potentially ruinous conflict. His mediation had established in 1493, a year after Columbus had landed in the Caribbean, a demarcation into zones east and west of an imaginary line running north-south a hundred leagues west of the Cape Verde Islands. The idea was to give Portugal Africa and the eastern trade and Spain what was found in the Americas. That the Portuguese knew more than they revealed about what lay over the Atlantic was suggested by Dom João's immediate dispatch of a delegation to the court of Ferdinand and Isabella at Madrid to renegotiate the deal. Portuguese persistence won out, and the following year Portugal and Spain signed a treaty at Tordesilhas that shifted the line much farther west, to 370 leagues west of the Cape Verde Islands. The new line now passed through the still theoretically unknown South American continent, so that when he was so surprisingly washed up on its coast six years later, Cabral naturally claimed the eastern part of the continent for Portugal. The legal questions had already been looked after.

————

Brazil's splendors are on such a scale that many are only visible from a distance. Once I spent several weeks flying into the continent, hopping from city to city as far as Manaus on the Amazon. The tangle of great silver rivers catching the light among the deep green absorbency of the forest canopy, then the water taking fire in the moments before sunset as the jungle turned into black velvet—this was something you could only know from the air. Flying is the only way to conceive the dimensions of Brazil and the only way to reach its many roadless settlements. The distances make planes an ordinary part of Brazilian life. Those who can afford them catch pancontinental flights like the local bus, as they do in North America and Australia, or grab an air taxi for shorter hops. Others have their own planes, light craft for getting around the farm, executive jets for getting from one meeting to another, helicopters for getting home to the gated community from the office. The little group of Brazil's rich are sylphs inhabiting a little airborne milieu out of sight of everyone else. Their world is far from check-in queues or lumbering mass transport planes, and its faintest earthly traces are the rooftop helipads and private landing strips, and even these lie far from profane eyes.

Air travel's glamour and convenience—and at higher levels its discretion—made planes a special object of desire for PC Farias. President Fernando Collor's first big privatization was of the airline VASP. The buyer was a friend and PC gave him $11 million for a share in it. They still didn't have quite enough to buy the airline outright, and then PC had the idea of getting a ten-year interest-free loan of $40 million from Brazil's state oil corporation, Petrobras; $30 million of it could be handed over as jet fuel. A ten-year interest-free loan, with rates running as they were, amounted to a gift of $40 million, and Petrobras said no. Then the telephone calls began.

The calls from PC came so insistently that the president of Petrobras had them recorded. PC called him a dozen times and visited his office twice. *You're creating a lot of difficulties,* PC said. Then Fernando's chief of cabinet, who was his brother-in-law, rang to express the president's *great interest in the VASP privatization's going ahead.* On a visit to New York, the head of Petrobras started getting calls from PC at his Park Avenue hotel. He refused to take the calls and his wife told PC he was jogging in Central Park. PC got annoyed. The Petrobras chief found himself under attack in the Brazilian press and accused of undermining the Collor Plan and the Brazilian currency. Seven months into Fernando's presidency, the head of Petrobras called a press conference, denounced PC's interference and resigned. Fernando expressed his satisfaction and said he had never *fitted in*. The fight had led to an item in the *Jornal do Brasil* revealing that *the man behind the campaign against the current president of Petrobras . . . is the mysterious PC Farias*. A reporter went to Alagoas to find out who PC was, and a weekly magazine published an article on him. The cover showed a terrible little black and white snapshot of a bald man with mustache and glasses, which was the only picture of PC anyone could find at that time. The magazine was offered money to suppress the article but refused, and other papers started to notice *the government's intrigues, lies and shady deals* and question *PC's rapid rise*.

Fernando's government disliked critics and soon showed its displeasure. The *Folha de São Paulo* was the most influential daily newspaper in Brazil. It was a rather dull broadsheet that took its own views very seriously and had been quite sharply critical of Fernando during the election campaign—even harder on Lula—though it had later supported Fernando's bank freeze. A platoon of armed police raided the paper during Fernando's second week in office, storming through its offices, seizing documents and looking for the owner. They said the raid was a search for fiscal irregularities but the paper felt it as intimidation. Five months later the *Folha* noted the government was handing out advertising contracts without calling tenders. The Brazilian government spent $500 million a year on advertising for the state owned banks and corporations and the contracts were in the gift of Fernando's private secretary, who was an old school friend of PC's from Alagoas. The secretary was feeding the contracts to small businesses who had worked for Fernando's election campaign, and when the *Folha* drew attention to this, Fernando sued. It was the first time a Brazilian president in office had sued for libel. Fernando was still very popular and the *Folha*'s editor was insulted in the streets of São Paulo and feared arrest. Curiosity about PC continued to spread.

Paulo Cesar Cavalcanti de Farias was an honest tax man's son from the interior of the Northeast. There were six boys and two girls and PC was the eldest of the eight. He was born in 1945 in the outback of Alagoas. Their father, whom the children respectfully addressed as *Collector,* worked all day in the local tax office and their mother made the children's clothes, kept house and did the cooking. She was deeply religious and helped their even poorer neighbors and kept her children's noses to their school books. At meal times they only spoke with their parents' permission.

Toward the end of the 1940s the family moved to the state capital, Maceió. The Farias boys all slept together in the attic of a little house and in the daytime they studied at the Marist Brothers college, half an hour's walk up the road, and played football in the street. Their mother wanted one of her boys to be a priest, another a lawyer and a third a doctor. When he was nine PC was enrolled in the seminary at Maceió to learn French and Latin and prepare to serve God. It was the only way a bright poor boy could get a decent education. By the time he was fourteen PC was giving private lessons to help the family. A social photo showed the teenage PC dressed in a black soutane with a wide sash, with a cigarette between his fingers. Soon after the photo was taken, PC's lack of a vocation was obvious to everyone and he switched to study law. He could not afford to go off to university in Rio or São Paulo or Recife, and enrolled in the little state university of Alagoas. There is no record of just when PC decided his father was a loser, but from the moment PC got out of the seminary the constant factor in all his wildly various undertakings was the promise they held out of upward movement. Most of PC's efforts were at making money, but the moneymaking was preceded by activities of another kind that suggested PC's first real interest was power, and that it was only later that he came to understand that power and wealth were more or less the same thing. One entailed the other, and knowing this made him comfortable in the shadows. PC needed recognition from people who mattered. He never sought the attention of the crowd.

He arrived at university in time for the military coup of 1964. While other students around Brazil organized resistance to the dictators, PC began his career as a militant of the right. As president of the students' organization, PC was one of the few allowed to vote in the *indirect* election for state governor of Alagoas, the only kind of election the military allowed, and in 1966 he voted for the winning candidate, who was a cousin of his father's. By the time he graduated at twenty-two, PC had a clerical job in the governor's office and told people he was the governor's private secretary, which opened a few doors. He did some outback legal work in the criminal area, and was paid for his services in crates of fruit and poultry from his subsistence farmer clients. He started selling telephone lines to drylands settlements on commission for the telephone company and discovered his talent as a salesman. He sold a lot of telephones and started making money. Being known, as PC made sure he always was, as a personal friend of the state governor was a big help in signing up new telephone subscribers as PC worked his way through the towns of the interior.

PC used the same talking skills as an announcer on a local radio station owned by the church. The studio was just by the cathedral in Maceió, on a square where people bought and sold used cars. PC and used cars were made for each other, and PC snuck away from the microphone to hang around the car mart. He left an old radio program tape playing on an eternal loop in the studio while he went off wheeling and dealing, trading cars for wristwatches. This was when they started calling him Little

Paulie Gasoline. The bishop of Maceió turned on Radio Palmares for background music during his snoozes after lunch, and realized after a while that he was hearing the same announcements and the same music over and over again. PC talked his way out of dismissal, obtained the bishop's pardon and went on dealing in used cars and working on the radio. Then he went into a serious used car dealership. A sugar planter put up the money and PC moved the cars. He moved on to a gas station and the Chevrolet dealership in Maceió. By 1970 PC had set up a Chrysler dealership that he parlayed into one of the biggest truck sellers in the Northeast of Brazil, his first really serious business. Two years later he added a tractor dealership. When Brazilian cars started running on sugarcane alcohol, PC sold the equipment for cane farming and distillation. But he always spent more than he made and life went on being a struggle, at least on paper. He bought a big black used Ford Galaxie and hired a driver. The driver wore a black chauffeur's uniform with a tie and cap and PC rode around Maceió in the back seat, holding up the financial pages of the papers, driver and passenger sweating like pigs in the tropical heat. PC kept the windows rolled up to simulate the air-conditioning he couldn't yet afford.

The metamorphosis of Little Paulie Gasoline into PC Farias did not happen overnight, and the new personal style evolved slowly. He started holding Friday night soirées, with girls flown up from Rio and the janitor acting as butler in a rented jacket. PC's own look was still based on black silk shirts, alternating with several others in brilliant colors, and the heavy gold crucifix nestling in the chest hairs. There was a lot more gold on the hairy wrists and the thick and unusually clumsy fingers. PC never learned to open a bottle unassisted. His hair started thinning early and he grew enormous sideburns in the early seventies manner. He had always been short and now his whole body was thickening fast as he made his way into the good life. In the words of someone from the Southeast who knew him later in life and knew his history and was nevertheless seduced by PC's silver tongue and not unsympathetic to PC's ferocious efforts to drag himself up from the dirt,

> PC was a special person in Maceió. Unlike others he could talk, he could persuade people, initiate projects. And he was reliable: he never failed to keep his word . . . He was a born capitalist, an ambitious entrepreneur, a man on the make in a wretchedly poor region, a shaky bookkeeper who knew his way around the bureaucracy and the law and knew how not to get caught . . . His goal was to be head of a rich family that owned diverse and powerful business interests, that was respected and politically influential.

As the lifestyle expenses rose, business did not always go well. The plantation of eighty thousand coconut palms seemed in deep trouble even with all the tax breaks from the state government. By 1983 PC was $7 million in debt and receivers were called in. But PC's creative accounting ensured that though he was insolvent in Brazil he had a lot of money in Panama. In 1985, after a ministerial inspection of PC's tractor dealership, the Brazilian attorney general's office laid twelve fraud charges against PC. The tax collector's son was charged with forging receipts and practicing tax evasion. In 1986 the earthmoving business folded and the next year PC's access to rural development funds was cut off. Yet he seemed to have more and more money to spend, despite the travails of his businesses. Which was why the authorities had been curious about his business activities in the first place.

PC's mother made sure he gave jobs to all his siblings, even when he wanted to sack them. *Shut your big mouth, Paulo, and do what I'm telling you,* his mother said, and PC did. He put one of his brothers through medical school in Rio and a specialization course in California. And through his partner in the motor show-room he got to know the Lyra brothers. The Lyras were two of the biggest sugar producers in Alagoas. They also ran several big air taxi companies and controlled a large part of the state's economy and its politics. PC made himself useful to the Lyras and under their auspices his business activities flourished, if not always seeming to. In 1984, just when his businesses were facing bankruptcy, he ran campaign finances for candidates favored by the Lyras, and as their bagman he got to know more people on the political and business scene of Alagoas. At this time he refreshed his acquaintance with a young deputy who represented Alagoas in the federal Congress, Fernando Collor de Mello.

Four years later, Fernando Collor and PC had developed a for-midable reciprocity when it came to furthering each other's interests, but the audience for their brilliant double act was still contained within a small circle in the tiny and obscure sugar and cattle state of Alagoas. When Fernando turned up at the headquarters of TV Globo in Rio at the end of 1988 to say he wanted to be president of Brazil and to ask for Globo's support, the founder and patriarch of the Globo media empire—and Globo ran the biggest TV network in the world outside the United States—was one of the few people in the rest of Brazil who knew who this young man was.

Roberto Marinho was immensely rich and powerful and—as practically a self-made man—a prodigy in Brazil. In 1988 he was eighty-three and had been an American-dollar billionaire for at least a decade. His father had begun his working life as a proofreader on the newspapers and founded *O Globo* as an eve-ning daily in Rio in 1926. There were at least a dozen daily papers in Rio in those days and it was no big deal. Three weeks later, twenty-year-old Roberto found his father dead on the bathroom floor from a heart attack. The son threw himself into reporting and then into running *O Globo* with maniacal energy. Roberto Marinho was a horserider, a spearfisher and a ladies' man, a smart journalist and a smarter entrepreneur. He made *O Globo* grow through the thirties, went into radio in the forties and television in the fifties, and used TV Globo and Radio Globo to promote his paper all around Brazil. In 1988 the weekday sales of *O Globo* were the second highest in the country and its Sunday sales topped all, and by then the paper was only a small part of the Globo empire. Roberto Marinho had a way of getting on with those in power. He got on especially well with the military and conspired in their coup of 1964. Interests coincided and Globo power grew mightily in the sixties and seventies, along with Marinho's personal clout. These were the years when TV Globo grew into the world's fourth biggest television network. Before the military there had been fewer than half a million television sets in Brazil, and when the regime faded in 1985 there were nearly twenty-seven million.

What Brazilians mostly watched on their sets were the soaps. Globo *telenovelas* brought together a vast and scattered audience of mainly illiterate people, gave a whole population stories to share and something to keep them quiet. Endless and anodyne dramas unwound on the Globo screens. Most of them were about conflicts over sex and money in immensely wealthy white families living in huge apartments overlooking Rio, which was the Globo city. Actors flounced into and stormed out of vast carpeted living rooms, collapsed or clinched on huge ivory Naugahyde sofas, quivered with emotion in close-up as they clutched a telephone receiver to their cleavage. The unfolding of the plots matched the weekly market research into audience response, which was partly why they felt so unstructured. They could be axed in days if popular interest fell, dragged out for years if people liked them. Individuals whose ratings fell were written out of the story overnight and new faces brought in. Fulminant brain tumors and car crashes and departures for the exterior were matched by returns from the dead—memory loss, the wrong body, whatever. The better a soap did, the longer it survived and the more completely it lost any form or meaning beyond the tiny peaks before each commercial break. These soaps were as far as you could get from the tightly wound clockwork mechanisms of American film or British TV. They went on and on forever, as nourishing as chewing gum, and their actors seemed to be chewing gum rather than feeling and speaking.

That a Brazilian soap became a river of flotsam carrying everything on its endless downward flow—that it lacked drama's elements of tension, conflict, resolution—seemed to reflect something you saw in all of the real Brazil's social relations, from the personal to the political. This was the avoidance of confrontation of any kind, an endless elasticity of evasion and spurious amiability. Did it reflect real life inside the Brazilian family, and that unusually complex mesh of promiscuity and repression that had lasted from the days of masters and slaves? Or the contemporary reality that the briefest confrontation with a stranger in the street might lead to a knife in the guts or a bullet in the head? Or did it derive from atavistic fears of a bloody rising by the underclasses? The ancestors of the penthouse families you saw in the soaps, the masters and their wives and children in the remote big houses on the sugar plantations, had often had their throats cut in the night by their insurgent slaves. Dramatic tension had only a relative interest in the television art of a society so many of whose immediate needs could be briefly resolved by a well-aimed bullet or a good fuck and none of whose other needs could ever be resolved at all.

That the tensions being avoided might have had some basis in race was obscured in the soaps by the absence onscreen of any black or colored person whatsoever. On one level, this was mere realism, there being about as many blacks living in penthouses as there were whites in the favelas, but it went beyond this. In the soaps, even the servants were usually white, which was not how things were in real life, and from the preponderance of blue-eyed blondes you might think, if it weren't for the suntans and the skimpy clothes, that the soaps were made in Scandinavia. And when in the nineties, after decades of penthouse drama, Brazilian TV started reaching outside the great cities and outside the immediate present for its material—when it started making drama series out of some of the lastingly popular regional novels of an earlier and rural Brazil—whole northeastern populations of farming settlements in Pernambuco and fishing communities in Bahia changed their color from black to white, or rather golden tan, in their translation to the screen. Art and social realism were fine if they pulled in advertising, but some of the unrealities of Brazilian television lay too deep to change.

The Globo soaps ran end to end from six till ten every evening and the only thing that interrupted them was the Globo evening news at eight. Globo news items were short, simple, carefully selected, heavily weighted to human interest and always presented by white people. As the military faded in the eighties, nothing changed on Globo screens or in the Globo command suites. Leaders of the tender new democracy wanted Roberto Marinho's approval and support more than anything. *I might be fighting with my army minister, but I won't be fighting with Roberto Marinho,* said the *indirectly* elected president of Brazil in 1985, who before he died chose as his minister of communications the owner of TV Globo transmission rights in Bahia. When little José Sarney took his place, the new ministry was vetted by Marinho before it was announced. Anyone looking to follow Sarney in 1989 would also want Roberto Marinho on his side and that was why Fernando came knocking.

Roberto Marinho knew Fernando because he had done business with Fernando's father, who had made most of his money from the TV Globo concession in Alagoas. Marinho suspected that Fernando's father had swindled him in property deals in Rio, and had lately sacked Fernando's elder brother Leopoldo from his management job in Globo, for misconduct. Now he balefully noted Fernando's fancy clothes and for a long time afterward referred to him as *the boy with the French cuffs*. All Fernando got from his first visit to Roberto Marinho was a certain amount of space thereafter on the Globo media, which mattered, however, since most of what most Brazilians knew about Brazil they learned from TV Globo.

Roberto Marinho's coolness toward Fernando didn't mean he was promoting anyone else for the presidency of Brazil. On the contrary, he was worried about the lack of a convincing candidate to stand against the resurgent left. Presidential elections were not really a Brazilian thing, and since there had been no popularly elected president of Brazil for forty-five years, the problem Brazil faced in 1989 of democratically electing its president was one nobody had ever dealt with. And by late 1988 inflation was running at a thousand percent a year and getting worse. The value of workers' wages had dropped by a quarter. The army had been breaking strikes, workers had been killed. In 1989 there was a two-day general strike in March that shut down most of the republic. There were more strikes in April, of dockworkers, metalworkers, schoolteachers. Stones were thrown at troops. Troops fired on strikers. Two million stopped work. The generals were getting restive again but it was too late to go back. Democracy was the future, Marinho realized, as long as the right president could be found, and the right president might be anyone but Lula.

In 1988 Roberto Marinho was newly in the grip of a sexual passion that had outlived fifty intervening years of marriage to two other women. Lily de Carvalho had arrived in Rio from France in the 1930s as a dazzling teenager and Lily and Roberto had danced together in the Golden Room of the Copacabana Palace, but Lily had married Roberto's friend instead. Now she was a widow with $150 million of her own and enchanting as ever, and Roberto Marinho was tired of his second wife's preoccupation with the communist menace and her dozens of cats. However virile and active, Marinho was now an old man. His mind was on the past in politics and love. He still thought the main danger facing his Brazil was the former governor of his own state of Rio de Janeiro. Leonel Brizola was a golden tongued populist who had tried to rally the armed forces against their generals in 1964 and was still a powerfully unsettling presence among many opposing nullities. Brizola would *tread on his grandmother's neck to be president,* as Lula rather spitefully said. But Brizola's influence on the left was quietly draining away. All year he had led in the opinion polls for next president, but now Lula equaled him at twelve percent and by the end of 1988 nobody else came anywhere near. From Brizola or Lula, Roberto Marinho felt that everything he had built up over the decades was increasingly under threat. Where was the leader who was going to defend the Brazil that mattered? Fernando Collor, an unknown politician from the second smallest, second poorest and most benighted state in the republic, unknown to the rest of the country, a spoiled playboy with no history to speak of, did not convince him at all.

When PC called the following year, Marinho agreed to see him readily enough, and listened intently as PC held forth on the candidate, the program, the campaign and the heavy costs of the campaign, and indeed Marinho had a great deal to say himself on these matters and offered his opinions generously. But whenever PC wanted to talk about money the conversation seemed to slither away into another channel. From his meeting with one of Brazil's richest men PC came away empty-handed, without actually having been refused and indeed without having been able to get around to making his request. It was PC's only failure in the year of the election. But what Roberto Marinho had to give as the owner of TV Globo was greater than money, and this in due course he gave to Fernando.

IV

Parrot Perch

A tribal leader's daughter living on the lower Amazon River became pregnant a long time ago. The angry chief used fire and duress to make her tell him the name of the father, but the girl insisted she had slept with no man. The chief was going to put his daughter to death, but a white man came to him in a dream and told him to stay his hand, because the girl was telling the truth and had never slept with a man. Nine months later she gave birth to a beautiful girl child who was white. Her tribe was amazed and so were the people of all the surrounding tribes, having never seen a white person, and they all came to look at Mani, which was the white child's name. Mani was walking and talking in almost no time and then, at the end of a year, without sickness or pain, she died. The tribe buried her according to custom in the ground below her own house. From the ground where they buried her a large-leafed plant sprouted of a kind the tribe had never seen before. It grew, flowered and bore fruit, and the birds who ate the fruit got drunk. The earth split open under pressure from its roots and when they dug they found that the white root the plant was growing from was the body of Mani. They tried the root and so began eating manioc, which in Tupi means *Mani's house.*

The white body of Mani had been providing the main food of the indigenous peoples in the newfound territory since the first millennium before Christ. Now manioc became the plant that fed the Portuguese and enabled the colony of Brazil to get through its first hard times. Pero Vaz de Caminha told the king of Portugal about it when he described the landing on Bahia in 1500 and Brazil's first governor issued an order for its cultivation forty-seven years later. Five hundred years later manioc is still— with rice and beans—the fundamental component of every Brazilian's diet. The *macaxeira* offered to Cabral's men, along with the feathered headdress, timber and fresh water, was the indigenes' first and greatest gift to the usurpers. The ever so slightly sweet macaxeira, or *aipim,* is like a slightly waxy potato with a few soft fibers running through it, and can be served boiled in big strips or used to make fries that make you wonder why you ever bothered with potato chips. The other main type of manioc is full of prussic acid and highly toxic, but the índios had developed a way of removing the cyanide, by grating the roots and soaking them in water and then forcing them into a big woven straw tube called a *tipiti* which drained off the poisonous juice. The secret of their food technology was the índios' second great gift to the invaders, and several millennia after they were first developed, tipitis are still used in Brazilian homes to make the poisonous manioc edible. The detoxified pulp could then be rolled out very thin and baked on a big flat stone to make *beiju,* a very thin and fine kind of unleavened bread still much eaten in Brazil, sometimes made with added coconut or cashew nut, and used to wrap a sweet or savory filling. But the Indios' most common treatment of the pulp was to roast it, grind it, roast it again until it became the coarsely powdered, sand colored and nutty tasting *farofa* that today is an invariable presence at every kind of meal on the tables of every social condition throughout Brazil, the unique and universal indicator of a Brazilian meal, *primary, irreducible, instinctive.*

Manioc flour became the first instance of that complex reciprocity of cultures that grew up between Brazil and Africa in the centuries of slavery. The slave ships stocked it for barter along with Bahian tobacco and cachaça when they sailed back to Africa, and soon in Africa manioc was planted around the slaving ports to supply food for the ships taking new prisoners to Brazil. Manioc grew as well in Africa as in Brazil, and its cultivation spread. Its high nutritional value soon made it one of Africa's staple foods. In Brazil the manioc was also processed as tapioca—another indigenous technique—and tapioca combined with northeastern sugar and the arts of Portuguese confectionery to produce the desserts and sweets that Gilberto Freyre wrote about with such profound emotion.

Farofa will be a part of any memorable Brazilian lunch, and it was of one in particular. One fine day in Recife, the hot skies immense blue and gold, one of those days when high pressure, low humidity and the mild breath of a coastal breeze make you feel coastal Brazil's is the most benign climate on earth, I had a Bangüê lunch. The Pátio was blinding at midday, the pastel houses bleached and flinging the light back into the empty space they surrounded. Crossing diagonally to the Bangüê, I raised the crowd of resident pigeons and intersected with Dona Lia arriving from the unfashionable baroque church of Santo Antônio dos Pretos, the black people's church around the corner where she spent hours on her knees every morning. Vavá was not in sight, but cheerful round-faced Jorge, who worked the lunchtime shift, waved me in. The Bangüê at midday was a restaurant and not a bar. The side tables were let down from the wall and all were laid with white cloths and cutlery. The sunlight outside and the expanse of white linen within made everything airier and lighter

Peter Robb

than it felt at night. Jorge brought a bottle of Antártica, freezing but not frozen, to the table by the sedan chair. It was *feijoada* day and to try the Bangüê's feijoada had been a deeply pondered intent.

The overhead fans were still, the window shutters flung wide open, and from the mild penumbra of the room the tiny houses across the square were fixed in brilliant detail. Framed in the tall open rectangles, the houses' bright pastel colors and slight irregularity of finish, the animation of people hurrying across the square with outflung arms, like jerky figures in a silent comedy, and the periodically upswirling pigeons were like details in the street scenes of a naïf painter. Brazilian naïfs—there were a lot of them—were maybe less naïf and more realistic than they seemed. I stretched my arm along a shaft of the sedan chair, worn smooth by slaves' labor, and waited for the meal which had its distant origins in the poorest circumstances of the slave quarters' fireplace.

In the mountainous parts of Portugal they still eat a dish of white beans and pork not unlike the French cassoulet, and a lot of Brazilian dishes have their origin in Portugal. Pork and beans tended to gravitate toward each other spontaneously and many rather similar slow cooked combinations are found all around those parts of the world where both are available. There is a lot of both in Brazil, only the beans are black or brown. This is the historical, culinary fact. The Brazilian myth is that the slave dish feijoada was first made from scraps from the big house kitchen, bits and pieces graciously conceded, or filched or rescued from the trash. The meat ingredients of a feijoada are various enough to imply a Saturday night special of hoardings made over the week. There are about a dozen kinds of beef and pork, fresh, smoked and salt, in a feijoada. The pig provides the animal's salted ears, sliced up and salted tails hacked into inch-long lengths, its trotters fresh and split down the middle, smoked bacon, salt bacon, pork ribs, pork loin, *paio* blood sausage and sweet seasoned linguiça sausage. The beef is jerky—*xarque*—and rump, chuck and smoked tongue. The meat components are endlessly variable. Even the beans vary by region. In Rio they use black beans and in the Northeast and São Paulo they use brown. The large fat black *feijão,* with its deep, deep, almost purple gloss—a shining aubergine black when cooked—and its firm consistency, is to me much more beautiful and tasty than the nondescript and somewhat mealy brown, which disintegrates more easily with cooking into a reddish paste. I believe that this day the Bangüê served a *feijoada carioca* with black beans rather than a northeastern feijoada with brown. This would have been odd and it may be a trick of memory and predilection that I recall it thus, and the room was shady.

Whenever I think of feijoada now my mind returns to this emblematic day. The deep earthenware pot that Jorge set down contained, under the lustrous nearly liquid shimmer of the cooked beans, pieces of pork and beef in a rare equilibrium of fresh, dried, smoked and salted in all their various tastes and textures, cooked long enough and carefully enough for each to have lent and borrowed something and reached a complex harmony in which all of the single components retained their own identity. This intimate reciprocity of the different elements is what a good feijoada is about. It is a curiously light dish whose subtlety belies the list of its own gross ingredients. It is a great instance of that transforming principle enunciated by Huck Finn, about to become a runaway boy in the company of Jim the runaway black slave, and escape among other things the miseries of poor white Anglo cuisine in which *everything was cooked by itself.* Always attentive to what he eats, Huck notes that *in a barrel of odds and ends . . . things get mixed up, and the juice kind of swaps around, and the things go better.* Stews are the great thing in Brazilian cooking—the delicately spiced inland stews of chicken and kid, the vividly African *moquecas* of the coast, made with anything from the sea, golden with palm oil and soft with coconut milk—but none of them enacts better than a good feijoada the magic that can happen in *a barrel of odds and ends.*

On the table, the glistening dark velvet of the feijoada shimmering in its pot was flanked by the deep emerald of the kale greens, shredded and sautéed in a little oil, hardly cooked and reeking of just warmed garlic, the big-grained Brazilian rice, the pale yellow of the farofa—farofa came into its own here, in dealing with all the densely laden juice, and the coarse roasted manioc flour was even more intrinsic to a feijoada than to all the other Brazilian dishes it enhanced—and the golden jewel of a many faceted fresh orange on its own plate, peeled with a sharp knife and looking, as its crystalline orange and whiteness glowed in the penumbra, like part of a Dutch still life. The white, the cream, the gold, the vivid green, the deeply purply black of the foods and the roughly glazed brown bowl and the tiny blaze of scarlet glowing from each of the tiny chilies forced into the narrow necked bottle of powerful pimenta made a profoundly harmonious whole to the sight. It was rich and various—the orange and green, and the elements they added in the way of mineral depth, ascorbic tartness, rough fibrousness to the complex whole was something usually missing in a Brazilian meal. Jorge brought a shot glass of neat cachaça and lime juice to go with the meal. In São Paulo they put orange juice and cachaça directly into the feijoada. I liked it like this.

———

New editions of the Bangüê's bill of fare were starting to appear more and more frequently. The list of dishes and drinks was printed and it always stayed the same but the spaces for the prices were left blank and typed in at each new updating by Dona Lia on her ancient manual typewriter. By September of

1990 the price updatings were almost weekly and the fiscal stability promised by the new president already forgotten. The printed words naming the dishes were becoming more familiar, and I realized that most of them were items of outback cuisine. Recife was on the sea, but apart from the reliable fried needlefish and a perfunctory *piece* of fried fish in the evening and a rather good fish stew, or *peixada,* for lunch on Friday, the produce of the sea did not figure in the normal offerings.

Recife itself was greatly populated by people from the interior. To people living through droughts that lasted for years on end the city on the coast was powerfully attractive. Unlike São Paulo in the south, Recife had almost nothing to offer the people who gravitated to it, beyond being easier to reach and less likely to destroy them. Even the temporary visitors who arrived with a truckload of produce for sale had a hard time flogging what they had grown for a street corner pittance, and were always being moved on by truckloads of council guards wearing baseball caps and armed with truncheons. Those who came with nothing, or with their children, found nothing, and these were the people I saw huddled in the church porches or around fires they had made in the public squares at night, and sleeping on flattened cardboard cartons. Sometimes when it rained at night, walking home and sticking to the covered pavements and arcades, you would see a thin hand or a dark foot protruding from under a piece of cardboard in the darkness as you were about to step on someone's bed. People brought their children here and left them, when they thought they were old enough to fend for themselves on the street. Other children came on their own.

In the worst times of the inland drought of 1970, the starving people who arrived in Recife from the interior had been helped by Dom Helder Câmara, the bishop of Recife, and he remarked, when he grew notorious as a friend of the dispossessed, that *when he fed the poor people called him a saint and when he asked why they were poor people called him a communist.* But Dom Helder was forced to retreat into silence and inaction by the new pope, John Paul II, and by the end of the eighties was in any case very old. After its great last stand with the people against the military in São Paulo, the engaged and human Roman Catholic Church in Brazil had become shrunken and inert under Wojtyla's deadening hand. Its influence was fading fast, although Brazil was still called the largest Catholic country in the world. The church of the first colonizers was ridiculed or ignored among the middle classes for its harangues against contraception, abortion and divorce and everywhere else it was being supplanted by proliferating evangelical sects.

Some of the Protestant churches were modest, austere and old-fashioned Baptist chapels where the ladies wore long dark dresses and hats, the men wore dazzling white shirts and dark jackets and the children had brilliant shoes and all clasped the Gospels bound in black leather. The newer ones celebrated fancier rites in temples the size of aircraft hangars and were run by organizations on the North American model, rich and powerful, highly organized, politically demanding and followed by millions. Unlike the Brazilian Catholic Church these offered prospects in the here and now as well as a hope of redemption in the afterlife, and for any candidate for government in Brazil it was more important to get the mass evangelical churches on one's side than to be limply endorsed by the Catholic hierarchy. African religions kept their powerful following in the old slave port cities of the Northeast and had a stronger hold on the minds of European Brazilians than outsiders found easy to realize. In the interstices Brazil pullulated with the adherents of every imaginable belief. Astrological determinism, New Age babble, self-help vacuities and psychologism of all kinds invaded the minds of those many millions of Brazilians who had neither a good education, strong cultural ties nor any immediate hopes in the real world. The land was full of crazies. I met a boy in Recife living in an abandoned house. *Are you a Believer?* he asked. His mother and father had been Believers, in some other city, and now they were dead. *Another Believer killed them.*

Vavá had no discernible religious interest—and was scathing about the church when I asked—and Lia prayed most days. It was a common enough division in marriage. They were themselves both from the interior of Pernambuco, and had gone south to São Paulo just after their son was born. Alexandre had grown up in São Paulo and was already a teenager when the family came back to the Northeast and settled in Recife. Vavá was intensely interested in other people, but years after being transformed in the Southeast from a shy northeasterner into a big city bookseller and art dealer, he still had to overcome a deep personal reticence. It took me a while to realize that the reticence had to do with his being not just a northeasterner but an inlander in origin, from a town on the edge of the high vast drylands where people were dry and laconic and tough. Somewhere inside, Vavá was still a *matuto,* a boy from the bush. He had been around a lot and knew a lot of people of all social conditions, but retained that modest reserve, and an economical social style that identified him as a drylander. That his was the best bar in town had everything to do with the kind of person Vavá was, combining Brazilian cordiality with northeastern reserve.

———

The interior drylands took up well over a million square kilometers, three-quarters of the entire territory of the Northeast. One in three Brazilians lived in the Northeast, but nearly all stayed in the lush littoral. The people of the drylands were a smallish minority, distinct in their appearance and their culture. The Brazilians' name for their drylands came from old Portuguese—my massive dictionary of Brazilian Portuguese described the name of the *sertão* as being *of obscure origin,* but it wasn't really. A *deserto* was a desert and a *desertão* a big desert, which was how the seafaring settlers saw the dry and scary interior. In time they dropped the prefix and often they made the word plural into *sertões* to match their sense of the new continent's endless hinterland. Beyond the green and well watered coast with its temperate sea breeze, and a higher middle zone that was good for grazing, one stony drought-ravaged wasteland receded into another, marked out by ranges of dry hills and waterless riverbeds. Like the name of Australia's outback, the word *sertão* was freighted with the sense of a world elsewhere, beyond human settlement and like the *never never* in some ways beyond understanding.

It was strange and bleak to the maritime people who settled Brazil and *clung to the coast like crabs.* Gradually it was sprinkled with human inhabitants. The índios, retreating from white disease, white weaponry and white projects to enslave them, retreated from their coastal forests to the highlands out of Portuguese reach. They were followed by the settler military, looking for slaves, and the settler priests, looking for converts. By the end of the seventeenth century the índios were gone even from the drylands where they had taken refuge. Índio Brazil remained strongly present in the Northeast and especially the drylands through sexual contact. The indigenous people mated first with white Portuguese settlers and later with the black slaves from Africa. The Africans, when they escaped, headed for the thinly peopled wilds of the interior as the índios had before them, and like the poor whites who were looking to stake a claim and make a living. The intermarriage of the three races was unusually complete and long lasting in the drylands and the people developed quite early into a distinct physical type as the compact, sharp featured, mahogany skinned northeasterners.

The slave hunters on their inland treks—sustained and fortified by manioc, which they planted and harvested as they went, and carried with them as the índios did on their war parties as *war flour*—were on the lookout for gold, as well as what Antônio Vieira, the índios' great champion among the Portuguese, called the *red gold* of indigenous slaves. Toward the end of the seventeenth century they found it, but farther south and not in the Northeast. They brought cattle with them as well as manioc, food on the hoof for long expeditions, and the cattle stayed. Stock trails were worn into the landscape and the interior was parceled into huge cattle properties, some of which were bigger than entire nations in Europe. The owners of these endless properties, the *colonels,* were the only embodiment of the state in this wilderness and they decided what the law was.

The colonels as individuals might or might not formally hold that rank in the national guard, a rank that back in the time of the empire had represented the formal authority invested by the state in the biggest landholder of any given part of the interior. Eventually they gave their name to the whole play of force by which people in the remoter parts of the Northeast were kept compliant. It lasted for a hundred years or more and after a while Brazilians in the south started talking in the newspapers and universities about *colonelism* as if it were a system of government rather than the arbitrary use of power by those who held the land and the water, people who had clout in the coastal capitals and in the south. Judge and police chief in any district each owed his job to the colonel, who was *lord of life and death.* Like their children who died of sickness or hunger, most of the men shot dead at the wells or in front of their mud huts by the colonels' armed enforcers on horseback had never legally existed in the first place.

The overweening power of the colonels went back to the first days of the colony. Some of them, in a contorted and attenuated way, could trace their property rights back to the very first days of settlement. It was 1530 when Dom Manuel of Portugal determined that his sailors and traders would have to push inland from the little enclaves they had dotted along the coast. Fortified coastal trading posts like these had given Portugal wealth without responsibility all along the African and Indian coasts, but they were useless in the densely forested Brazil of hunter-gatherers. In Brazil there were no trade routes, no manufactured goods, no middlemen. If the Portuguese wanted to make a go of their *new world in the tropics,* they would have to settle it.

The coastal Tupi had been more than ready to trade brazil-wood, the tree whose trunks yielded a red dye that was a hot item in early-sixteenth-century Europe. Red was the glamorous color that century, and brazilwood was particularly sought after in France, even though the dye it contained was thin and not very stable. The Tupi used to cut the trees down and bring them to the ships. They would have traded anything for metal cutting tools and firearms. But the trees soon thinned out and nothing else offered quick returns. Even gold was going to have to be mined. There were no Incas or Aztecs in Brazil. Dom Manuel or his advisers divided the newfound land into fifteen horizontal strips, starting at the coast and ending wherever Spanish rights began. He offered perpetual rights in each such captaincy to a selected member of the aristocracy having the will and the resources to develop a colony. One of the strips was Pernambuco, inland from Olinda, and the next one south was Bahia, inland from the city of Salvador on the Bay of All Saints. Only two captaincies made a go of it in the early days, the investment was so heavy and the returns so slow. The colonies never seemed to get started. Pernambuco was one of the two that did, and the secret of its success lay in Europe's craving for sugar.

The most productive of all the sugar growing areas in coastal Pernambuco was the part called Alagoas in the south, just above the mouth of the mighty São Francisco River, which wound for thousands of kilometers through the inland and as it neared the coast became the border that separated Pernambuco from Bahia. For a long time Alagoas, so called for its lakes and lagoons, produced more sugar than almost anywhere else in Brazil, although it was a very small region. Its productiveness of sugar promoted it to the status of a province and it finally became the second smallest state in the federal republic of Brazil. The only smaller state was Sergipe, just over the river, chipped out of the huge state of Bahia. Alagoas was not all coastal sugar estates. It had its inland component of dryland whose landowning colonels ran cattle and disputed power in the state with the sugarcane plantation bosses of the coast.

Pernambuco's interior was where Lula came from, which was why he looked so at home in the streets of Recife. But Lula's identity was formed in an utterly different world and it was a long time before he looked back to the place and the people of his origins. Luis Inácio da Silva—*Lula* came years later—was born in a tiny shack in an indeterminate area the locals called *Varzea Comprida,* or Long Plain, in a shallow river valley outside the town of Garanhuns. He was the seventh child of a dirt-poor farmer and he was conceived and born on the edge of the drylands during the bitter drought of 1945. The child Lula grew up fed by his mother on a little manioc meal mashed into some remains of cold coffee.

Aristides Inácio da Silva, being unable to feed his wife, Euridice, and the six small children who were about to be seven, had walked out on them a fortnight before Lula was born. Aristides traveled three thousand kilometers to the south on the back of an open tray truck in search of work. He found it as a dock-worker loading coffee sacks in the port city of Santos. Just south of São Paulo, Santos was one of Brazil's first European settlements and São Paulo's outlet to the sea. There Aristides took up with a new woman, who happened to be his wife's cousin, and together they had two children, four by some accounts. Some years later he took his newer wife and the new children back to Long Plain for a visit. Euridice now learned about the new southern branch of the family, and the five-year-old Luis clapped eyes on his father for the first time. Aristides stayed in Long Plain for three weeks and then went back to Santos, taking Euridice's two eldest children with him and leaving Euridice pregnant with their eighth.

A while later, Euridice had a letter from down south, inviting her and the other children to join Aristides in Santos. At the end of 1952 she loaded the six remaining children onto the back of a flatbed truck driven by a neighbor from Garanhuns—one of the locals who made a living transporting the migrants to the south—and they spent the next thirteen days on the back of the truck traveling down to Santos. Trucks like this, with their tray perimeters finely painted with brightly colored lines, were called *parrot perch* trucks and all the passengers traveled standing on the tray, clustered together and clinging to a wooden support in the center. They can be seen at a distance on the dirt roads of the drylands, kicking up a cloud of red dust as they transport little knots of laborers to work, guests to weddings, buyers and sellers to markets.

This particular truck's arrival in Santos caused some consternation. Aristides had sent no invitation. The letter to Euridice had been forged by their eldest boy, who was missing his mother. Aristides intended to go on living with Euridice's cousin, although he also made Euridice pregnant again another couple of times. He had more children by her cousin too. By the time he died in 1978 Aristides da Silva was the father of twenty-three children, ten by Euridice and thirteen by her cousin. The domestic situation in Santos became a little tense or messy after four years of the extended family's presence in the same city, and in 1956 Euridice broke away and took her children to São Paulo. In the great city they lived in a single room at the back of a bar, and shared its toilet with the customers. Luis, who was eleven when they moved, had been working on the streets since he was seven, like millions of other small children in Brazil, selling oranges and peanuts and homemade tapioca sweets. He had got some schooling too, and learned to read the year before. In São Paulo Luis got his first full-time job, working for a dry cleaner. It didn't last, and the boy then worked as a shoeshiner, again like millions of young Brazilian boys, treading the fine line that separated subsistence from indigence, lugging a heavy wooden implement box and customer footrest on a shoulder strap around the hot and polluted public spaces, working the bars and the restaurants and the bus stops and the park benches. He got some casual work in an office and felt the first pangs of embarrassment about inviting any of his friends to the room where they lived at the back of the bar. There was no chair for the friend to sit on and Luis realized his family was poor.

Then he got a real job, in a factory that made nuts and bolts, which was something for a thirteen-year-old northeasterner. The migrants from the Northeast soon discovered that they were not much liked in the new industrial Brazil of the south. Like Sicilians in Milan and southern blacks in Chicago at the same time, they aroused obscure feelings of shame and resentment. Brazilians still ignore the history of these internal migrants. Nobody recognizes what they gave, and what they went through—or what they still do, because the Northeast still provides the labor that fuels the growth in the south. The lives of Brazil's earlier immigrants from Europe are recorded and celebrated in histories and soaps as part of the national epic, but not those of the newcomers from within Brazil itself. A new life for the huddled and suffering masses from *elsewhere,* such as Brazil once offered, is one thing, but to recognize the hunger and desperation that drove the internal migration from the Northeast, and the human cost of that displacement, still causes unease. Yet the northeasterners who went south were tens of millions and the public and private glories and horrors of Brazil today are founded on this vast movement of people.

At the end of his first day Luis ran home in his rusty grease smeared metalworker's overall and showed his mother his dirty worker's hands. He recalled this many years later. The general record holds little about Luis's mother. Like the earlier fact that her seventh child had managed to snatch a basic literacy from the least promising of circumstances, the image of the thirteen-year-old in his work clothes is a picture of the skill and determination that Euridice, the woman from the northeastern bush who came south by mistake, deployed to pilot her ten largely fatherless children through the new industrial jungle of São Paulo. And given her silence and his reticence, the image may stand for a great deal. The factory shift was from seven in the morning until seven at night, or from seven at night until seven in the morning. It was during the night shift once that another apprentice worker who was holding back the blade of a lathe while Luis changed a bolt fell asleep at the machine. The blade slipped forward and sliced off the little finger of Luis's left hand. But Luis trained over three years as a lathe operator himself, and got work at one of Brazil's biggest engineering companies on the outskirts of São Paulo, where the car assembly plants were. That year Luis was twenty and it was 1966, two years after the military coup.

He was now a fully paid up member of São Paulo's industrial

working class and his interests were women and football. The military coup in Brazil did not heighten any sense in him that he belonged to a class of people the military had in its sights. Neither did it change his vague sense that the industrial unions, the government run unions set up in the thirties, were run by crooks. Luis was still a boy from the bush, with a deeply conservative rural northeasterner's wariness of the social ways of the industrial south. He clung to his past for a long time. His whole family was like that. The Northeast was like that. *We thought . . . they were only crooks . . . all the leaders were crooks.* An elder brother called José was a unionist and belonged to the underground Communist Party, but he was the only one in the family like that. They called him Brother Chico because he was like a monk with his pudding basin haircut and his devotion to the cause. The others argued with José when they were drinking cachaça. *We thought . . . my brother was crazy to belong to the union . . . we didn't want to hear about it.* It was four years before José convinced his younger brother to take out a union card. Luis dragged his feet. *I was a lathe operator. I was getting good enough pay and I had a girlfriend. I wanted to play football. I wanted to go out dancing. I didn't want to know about union things.* This was in 1968.

This was the year murder and torture became routine in the government of Brazil. Luis went on happily. He married his girlfriend, who worked in one of the textile factories, and she was soon pregnant. At the end of her term she went into a local hospital to give birth, with such attention as a factory girl could expect, and she and her child both died while she was in labor. Nobody had noticed that she had hepatitis, which killed them. The other thing that happened in 1969 was that José put the hard word on his brother again. This time José wanted him to join his slate for the elections to the local leadership of the metalworkers' union. Luis at length and reluctantly agreed to stand for the union directorate. He won a place and won it again in 1972. But he didn't follow José into the Communist Party. Luis was not a political person.

Luis kept his head well enough down for the president of his union, a labor boss who was very much a company man, to nominate him as a candidate for the succession three years later. The workers called the union boss a *pelego,* or saddle blanket, for his situation under the rider's rump and on the mule's back. Sociologists called a corporatist union boss an *urban substitute for the colonel.* The boss candidate Luis had not yet spoken at a big meeting, didn't even know how to use a microphone, and was sufficiently self-aware to suspect the departing president of wanting to shed a retrospective glow on his tenure by having an incompetent follow him in office. Nevertheless, with such an imprimatur the candidacy was bound to succeed and it did. The untried new man won ninety-two percent of the vote.

One of the early perks of office was a union trip to Japan. On his way home, stopping over in the United States, Luis learned that the military had arrested his brother José as a *sub-versive.* A union lawyer advised him to stay in the States until the heat went off. But Luis didn't like American food, which lacked rice and black beans and farofa and was in any case disgusting, and went straight back to São Paulo. He seemed galvanized by José's arrest and abruptly shed his anxieties about his own security, his job, his family. He said, *I lost my fear.* Charged up, he and some other young activists set out to kick some life into their cowed and compliant union. To get the metalworkers involved, they organized union football championships—factory teams against union leadership. Before the matches Luis talked for five minutes and after the game there was beer and a barbecue. They transformed the leaflets they gave out to factory workers, adding cartoons and comic strips and things people wanted to read. The handouts stayed in pockets and were no longer crumpled up and chucked away at the factory gates. The leaflets named names when factory supervisors started victimizing workers. They talked about the here and now in a lively concrete way and were different from the grimly programmatic clandestine leaflets José the communist had earlier pressed into Luis's hands.

Over the Andes in Chile, South America's oldest parliamentary democracy was destroyed in 1973 by the conspiracy of generals whose *caravan of death* was now picking out and exterminating the leaders of organized labor. It is not clear how far knowledge of the tortures and killings going on in that other world of the exterior penetrated São Paulo's industrial belt. Brazil was still isolated in its own vastness, a strangely self-absorbed and self-referring universe of its own, cut off from its Spanish-speaking neighbors by its different language, its different racial history, its different culture. Even in 1976 when Videla and the Argentinian generals, even closer to home, began their *dirty war* on workers and students, Luis and his mates went blithely on, unaware or unafraid of the danger that Brazil's own generals might decide to follow suit and go for broke.

What changed in the union being led by Luis was that the workers now took their claims straight to the labor tribunal and ignored the government's union federation. In 1976, for the first time ever they won a small wage raise. The new young union leaders were still benignly treated in the closely censored media, since they were assertive and unorthodox but not *communists.* When Luis stood for reelection in 1978 he ran on his record and won a slightly improbable ninety-eight percent of the vote. He *was still very thin and wore flares* and his thick black curly hair hung in long waving ringlets like tentacles and people started calling him *Lula,* which meant *Squid.* Lula put on a suit and tie and invited the regime's state governor and the army commander to his inauguration, both of which moves upset his union friends.

If Lula's awareness of the way Brazil worked seemed to have its radical inconsistencies, it was because he contained multitudes. He was not predictable. He was not sectarian. He was not an ideologue.

———

Sugar had run in the blood of Fernando Collor's family, but the sweetness was long gone. As the nineteenth century turned into the twentieth, more and more of the old sugar estates of northeastern Brazil were bankrupted and the big houses lay abandoned by their masters. The owner of the Little Waterfall plantation in Rio Largo, not far from Maceió in Alagoas, was ruined at the end of the Great War in Europe. His eighteen-year-old son, who had grown up on the sugar estate, went south to Rio with the money left from the sale of his father's land sewn into his underpants by his mother. Arnon de Mello studied law until the money ran out and then he worked as a journalist in Rio until his paper's offices were burnt down when the dictator Getúlio Vargas took power in 1930. He was smart and rose fast and in 1939 married the daughter of the dictator's minister of labor. When their second son was born ten years later, Arnon and Leda called him Fernando. Fernando's maternal grandfather, Lindolfo Collor, was the son of an immigrant German shoemaker. Brazil's very first labor minister, he had drafted the laws that created the government's industrial trade unions. The Brazilian government realized rather late that labor matters could no longer be left to the ministry of agriculture, and the corporatist—or fascist—labor laws drawn up by Lindolfo Collor in the thirties would last until the metalworkers' strikes in São Paulo at the end of the 1970s. Encouraged into politics by the example of his wife's father, in 1950 Arnon de Mello went home and ran for governor of Alagoas. Fernando was one year old.

The Northeast, unlike the Southeast, was not industrializing. It was falling further and further behind, and was still ruled by colonels whose understanding of politics was that when it was election time you took your peasants to the polling station and told them what to do. The current governor belonged to another family of ruined sugar planters, a wild and brutal clan who had become a political dynasty. One of them had been the dictator's war minister and his siblings ruled the state one after the other and expected to go on forever. Arnon de Mello arrived with a snappy jingle and the state's first ever election posters in full color; meet and greet and baby kissing in country towns where once the candidates went with bullwhips; a comic strip campaign bio with a brightly colored cover. He handed out campaign calendars, campaign pencils, signed campaign photos as the loudspeakers belted out the campaign jingle. He was in the papers, he was on the wireless. He ran campaign film shows in the sharp dry open air of the outback towns. He bought votes with spades, hoes, knives and the promise of the Singer sewing machine which went around with the candidate on the back of the campaign truck. Arnon won handsomely and the loser was shot four months later by a former congressman whose parents had been murdered. It was nothing new, and there would be another nine hundred political murders in Alagoas while Arnon de Mello was governor. The killings went on all over the state. A colonel in his seventies was stabbed to death by the military police. A former governor's grandson was shot in an ambush. A big landowner was killed by the police chief. A religious leader giving trouble was murdered by landowners' men. Arnon bought up the main opposition paper and set the police on the others. There were no public works. Six years later Alagoas was back in the hands of the defeated rivals and Arnon went back to making money in Rio.

Business was good and Arnon moved with the smart and the

very rich. He did property deals with Roberto Marinho, who owned the newspaper *O Globo*. They built Rio's first shopping mall together in Copacabana and it was opened by the president. In Alagoas Arnon kept his paper and added a radio station. In 1962 he was elected to the Senate in Brasilia. His old and hated rival was already installed and threatened to *fill his mouth with lead*. The new session in January 1963 opened with a shootout between the two senators from Alagoas. Arnon missed his target and killed another senator but he was imprisoned only briefly, and the movers and shakers in Rio still did business with him, and greeted him affably in the Jockey Club. Behind his back they raised their eyebrows and called him *the gunman,* which always got a laugh. The son of the ruined sugar planter, after his brilliant early days in Rio, his socially consolidating marriage and his lucrative property deals, was now marked as a northeasterner. The man *who had once shone in looking good in Rio was dragged down to the brutality of the land he came from. His social rise was stopped in its tracks.*

He concentrated on business. In the twenty-one years after military dictatorship began in 1964, the number of Brazil's television stations went from 14 to 150 and most of them belonged to Roberto Marinho. Arnon opened the first television station in Alagoas and transmitted Globo's programs. He became the media boss of Alagoas. His three sons and two daughters were now grown up. The sons were grossly indulged in the manner of rich boys in Brazil. The eldest soon showed himself dishonest and unreliable as well as incompetent, and dynastic hopes devolved on Fernando. He had much in common with his elder brother, but was more personable and more intelligent and in 1975 Fernando made a brilliant marriage to eighteen-year-old Lilibeth Monteiro, whose father owned one of the biggest industrial conglomerates in Brazil. The wedding party was held in the art deco splendor of the Copacabana Palace hotel, where the beautiful people of Europe and America came to holiday, and Fernando started being seriously noticed in Brazilian high society. *Baby* Monteiro de Carvalho was delighted with his stylish new son-in-law. The Monteiros had the newly elected governor of Alagoas to lunch in Rio and the governor made Fernando Collor de Mello mayor of Maceió. The family idyll soured when Fernando needed money and tried to sell his father-in-law some of his own family's real estate for a lot more than it was worth. *The kid's trying to take me in. I'm an experienced businessman and old enough to be his father,* Baby said. The marriage broke down into ugly domestic violence and Lilibeth flew off to Paris.

Fernando promoted Maceió as a tourist destination, which involved building a lot of hotels on the beach and fixing some of the terrible roads. Beautiful people from the south passed through town as freeloaders almost as often as Fernando flew south to the greater glamour of Rio. His last act as mayor in 1982 was to take on five thousand new municipal employees. *All votes for me,* he said, looking down on the endless queue of newcomers from an upper window. *Employment for electoral ends* was forbidden and Fernando, who was standing for the federal Congress, got in serious trouble with the military dictators in Brasilia. His successor as mayor had to ask for federal help to fix the mess he found in the city's accounts. *This boy ought to be in jail,* remarked the minister as he went over Fernando's financial records. But Fernando was elected to Congress easily and within a year his father, Arnon, was dead.

At a coming out ball in the remote interior of Alagoas Fernando had met fifteen-year-old Rosane Malta, daughter of the colonel who owned the cattle land around Big Scrub, high in the bone-dry inland where cattle and goats wandered through the town streets. The Maltas were the impoverished remnants of a dynasty that a hundred years before had run the state. In 1950 they had backed Fernando's father when he ran for governor and on the morning of the vote three of the Maltas were clubbed down and shot dead in the street by the opposition's hired killers. Fernando was linked to the Maltas by spilt blood and he liked fifteen-year-old Rosane enough to overlook her uncouthness. She was nineteen when they married in 1984. Fernando's family despised Rosane, who dished out as good as she got. In 1987 Fernando became governor of Alagoas and they lived in the Palace of the Martyrs in Maceió, built a hundred years before by Rosane's great-uncle, a governor who was twice chased out of it by howling mobs. PC, who was already in charge of the financial side of Fernando's life, made sure all their personal expenses were charged to the state government. While Fernando was governor, a candidate for mayor of Rosane's hometown displeased the Malta family and was shot dead in the back of the head by Rosane's younger brother and her uncle, and a young cousin of Rosane's killed someone else in Maceió the following year. Fernando finessed both of these awkward moments, and soon there were more than fifty Maltas on the government payroll.

It was Fernando's younger brother Pedro who had introduced PC Farias to Fernando. Pedro's wife was the daughter of one of the biggest sugar refining families in Alagoas and João Lyra was about to transform his economic power into political clout. Yet even the Lyras could be embarrassing in the way of the Northeast's ruling families. When a sergeant of the Alagoas military police was shot dead in an ambush some years later, João Lyra was named as the man who ordered the murder. Lyra had put a tap on his wife's phone because after thirty-six years of marriage he thought she was having an affair. He played the family a recording of her conversation with the sergeant. *Just look what your mother's planning to do,* he told them. The sergeant's killing caused some indignation locally because João Lyra himself was known to be having an affair of his own at this time with his nephew's wife, who was twenty years younger than he was.

When Pedro married Thereza Lyra toward the end of 1980, at a little wedding which brought together five thousand of the two families' very closest friends—a further list of two thousand people Fernando wanted to impress politically having been rejected as compromising the intimacy of the occasion—the bride's father invited PC to be the bride's sponsor. The beautiful young bride was startled by the sight of her godfather—who *was* this little bald man with the gold identity bracelets and the sideburns?—but João Lyra wanted to do PC a favor in return for services lately rendered as political bagman. He was helping PC raise his social profile.

Fernando so admired PC's way with money that he was prepared to overlook the white suits and silk shirts when he ran for governor in 1986. PC kept the campaign money pouring in. Salaries were paid, planes were hired, the TV ads went out— PC got Fernando elected governor of Alagoas and João Lyra senator in Brasilia at the same time. Fernando had significant and growing lifestyle requirements and the wonderful thing about PC was that he looked after the money without ever wanting to explain what he was doing, or how or why. Fernando began grooming PC into an acceptable associate, or at least a presentable one, just as he was grooming Rosane to be a presentable wife.

V

Below the Equator

An English traveler in eighteenth-century Brazil recorded in amazement and exasperation that every time he asked one of his Brazilian hosts about the way things worked in the New World, a black slave would be summoned to provide the explanation. The indolence and ignorance of Brazil's plantation masters in other than sexual things matched the sexually repressed indolence of their wives. In few places in the world was working your way so little valued as in Brazil. In the continent's original times it was natural. What else could you expect in a country which filled all human needs so gloriously? The warrior hedonism of the hunter-gatherer peoples who lived in the great river basins and the coastal forests flowed from nature's invitation to a prudent improvidence.

Then the Europeans landed and in the sixteenth century the idea of a golden age again gripped the European imagination, as strongly it had in antiquity. News of the people who inhabited the *brave new world* and were *only wild in the sense that we call fruits wild when they are produced by nature in her ordinary course* delighted Shakespeare and Montaigne. The idea that people might live with no constraints other than nature's was overlaid with tormented Christian notions of life before the fall, of sexual innocence and natural plenty, life defined by the absence of war, guilt, money, work, and the newfound world sowed the intellectual seeds of a newly non-Christian life. The freedoms of the New World's native peoples were, however, strictly a conceit for distant Europe. In Brazil itself the índios were more practically seen by the Portuguese colonists. The women were seized as marvelously available sexual partners, the men as a great source of slave labor. Hopefully the locals would also lead the colonists to the gold that would make a golden age for Portugal.

The Portuguese were doing well at overseas trade with African and Asian countries but making anything of the utterly different Brazil was going to be a long haul. As traders they had never planned to do the work themselves, or live permanently at the supply source. Portugal had a tiny population and Brazil was a huge territory lacking transport, communication or housing, even a reliable food supply. To colonize Brazil the Portuguese needed labor. The hunter-gatherer peoples of Brazil were not the answer, though the Portuguese did their best to make them change their ways. A quarter or half a million indigenous people were enslaved on the sugarcane plantations of the Northeast that replaced the forests where they had freely lived. In the first two centuries of the sugar industry, one in three of the slaves being worked to early death was índio. On the sugar estates the índios were then annihilated by the infections the Portuguese had brought from Europe, Asia and Africa. Epidemics of plague and smallpox and the common cold wiped out the tens of thousands of índio slaves on the sugar plantations of Bahia, and then the sicknesses moved north into Pernambuco and killed off the workforce there. The foreign diseases penetrated deep into Brazil's forests, and uncounted índios died out of sight. The dying gasped for breath for burning lungs as respiration failed. Stinking worm-riddled flesh fell from the bones of those who had lately seemed the handsomest and healthiest and maybe the happiest people in the world. The dead were too many for the living to bury.

Survivors were converted and herded into the Jesuits' fortified villages, Christians of a kind and slaves of a kind too, forced into calico smocks, sexual abstinence, hymn singing and an unpaid regime of crop raising and domestic service, rented out by the Jesuits to the lay population. The missionaries attenuated the suffering and prolonged the death of a people. They fought with the landowners and slave owners and imposed their own miseries in the name of saving souls. Demographically and economically, the indigenous Brazilians quite suddenly ceased to count. Their great defender among the Portuguese in the seventeenth century, the eloquent Jesuit Antônio Vieira, was so appalled by their enslavement and genocide that he came—like Las Casas in the Caribbean before him—to be an advocate of enslaving Africans and shipping them to Brazil. It seemed the lesser evil. Africans were tougher.

The transatlantic slave traffic was already under way. For the colonists African slaves were the perfect solution to their labor problems. Portuguese traders were already doing business with African slave dealers and slaves shipped from West African ports were being landed in Brazil within fifty years of Cabral's arrival. Over the next three hundred years four million Africans, maybe more, were shipped across the Atlantic into slavery in Brazil—seven times the number of African prisoners sold into slavery in North America. Millions of others died at sea before they reached Brazil. Most of the Africans were young men and boys who would die before they were thirty. The slave owners of Brazil were universally pleased with African strength and the African capacity for hard labor, but since the slaves died young and had no children, their owners were in constant need of replacements. For the Africans disease was not the main cause of death. It was the way they were made to live. It was the work they had to do.

The shipping of slaves from Africa to America was such good business for so long because in Brazil it was cheaper for sugar plantation owners to work young Africans to death in a few years and then buy new ones. A new slave, in the great age of sugar, earned back his cost price in a little over a year, and from then until he collapsed and died or was killed by design or accident he represented pure profit. The world's craving for sugar was insatiable and Pernambuco was soon the richest producer in the world. Maintenance costs were minimal, though the Africans were not a docile workforce on the Brazilian plantations. They knew they had little to lose. Their owners, as the Jesuits complained, at the slightest annoyance *threw their slaves alive into the furnace or killed them in various barbarous and inhumane ways.* Some of the slaves sabotaged the sugar production machinery. Others just ate dirt like the índios and waited for the end. Sometimes a plantation's Africans rose up together, hacked their overseers and owner to pieces and torched the place. And fled into the forest. They were without women for the most part. Imports of African women were as slow to start as the settlement of Portuguese women in Brazil. After a time the master's big house became bigger and children arrived and female slaves were needed to breast-feed them and clean and sew and cook the big meals the master's family consumed. Slave women themselves were almost useless for breeding. Their fertility rate was low and in any case breeding slave children made no economic sense, even when the children survived childhood. It cost far more to keep a black child for its first ten years than it did to buy a freshly unloaded healthy adult male ready to be put to work. The increase in Brazil's population of African slaves came entirely through imports, and the profit margin for the traders kept imports well ahead of the attrition rate as the economy expanded.

Brazil's was by far the largest system of slavery in the New World, and slavery lasted longer in Brazil than it did anywhere else. The British pressed to end it for years and finally got their way through the naval power of their empire. British control of the oceans and British control of the Brazilian economy made it relatively easy to ensure that the transatlantic trade in Africans was shut down in 1850. Final abolition within Brazil came in 1888, without a civil war of the North American kind or indeed any obvious social or economic trauma at all because slavery had lasted until the massive free emigration from the poorer parts of Europe. Arriving from Italy, Spain, Portugal and Germany, the newcomers were often so shocked by the conditions they found— slave owners took time to learn how to relate to free labor—that some European governments banned immigration to Brazil until things improved. The new immigrants nearly all settled in the south—it was the time of the coffee boom—and it was they who created Brazil's urban commerce and its late industrialization. Their immigrant hard work and their commercial expertise created the concentration of wealth in the city and state of São Paulo, but they never transformed the country's politics in a comparable way.

Power in Brazil stayed in the hands of the landowners, the exporters of sugar, gold, coffee, beef and rubber. Each state in Brazil was run by a small group of intermarried families. They were the people who a few years earlier had run their estates on slave labor and they still, in the remoter parts of the country—the coffee estates of the south, cattle runs in the drylands of the Northeast and the rubber plantations of the Amazon—kept the people working for them dirt poor and serflike in their dependence. Most of the northeasterners who went south left rural misery for the urban poverty nesting within the Southeast's huge industrial wealth. The landowning families dominated the military high command, and even the career officers who rose through the ranks identified with the ruling caste and were ready to step in with guns whenever its interests seemed threatened. As they had, with a big nudge from the United States, in 1964.

The way Brazilians lived was transformed in the middle of the twentieth century and nothing changed in the patterns of power. The landowners' club let in the new industrial wealth, but Brazil remained a society in which most people lacked representation. Whether it was old money or new money whose voice was currently being heard in the capital made little difference to most Brazilians. Neither the agricultural nor the industrial working people in Brazil were able to form their own workers' organizations, nor did they ever form political parties to represent their interests in government. The absolute newness of Lula in Brazil, so easy to miss from outside, was the more amazing for being twofold. He led the making of Brazil's first free and autonomous workers' union movement and he then led the formation of the first ever mass political party to articulate the larger needs and hopes of those working people—and of Brazil's tens of millions of dispossessed—in representative government. There was a lot of ground to make up. Brazil was still a rural slave society when such rights were being hard won in the industrial societies of North America and Europe, and nearly a century after the end of slavery, labor in Brazil was despised because it was still so cheap.

———

Slaves who escaped in the early days found that the forested vastness of the Brazil lying beyond the narrow coastal strip which was being cleared and cultivated afforded great refuge away from roads and settlements. The cost of pursuit and recapture of individual slaves weighed against the owners and the state, and laid bare the weakness of the masters' forces of control.

They could hardly send their slaves after the fugitives. Quite early, the dreadful fear of a mass revolt by the African slaves began to lurk in the minds of the Portuguese landowners. The fear lasted for centuries. There were so many Africans, and so few Portuguese. By 1600 there were already twenty thousand African slaves on the sugar estates of the Northeast, and in the next fifty years their number more than doubled. Precautions were taken. Slave owners mixed members of as many different ethnic groups as possible on their estates, people from different parts of Africa, with different languages, beliefs, traditions. It was much better for the owners if the only language the slaves all understood was the basic Portuguese in which they took their orders. Soon there were so many slaves and so many Portuguese slaving outposts along the African coast that the ethnic mix was easy. Consumer preference played its part. Some Africans were more docile, some harder workers, some more disease resistant. Toughness and troublemaking unfortunately went together. The sensible landowner preferred a blend of *pieces,* or *items,* as the Africans were called in the account books, and the high attrition rate among the *pieces* allowed for fine-tuning of the supply flow.

When slaves did escape into the wild, one African fugitive was likely to have no more in common with his fellow than an Englishman on the run might have with a Russian in a country foreign to both. There was also this difference for the Africans, that while the índios, fleeing forced labor and Christianity, headed deeper into a country they had known forever—every animal and bird, every plant, every fish, every insect, the flowing of the water and the tremors in the skies—the Africans were as far out of their element in Brazil as the Europeans were. But they did escape. Surviving in the wild was easier than surviving on the sugar plantations. Enough Africans escaped to form communities in the bush, and these communities became a pole of attraction for the Africans who remained enslaved on the plantations.

By the early seventeenth century the Portuguese were doing so well out of sugar that the rising Protestant Dutch, in the form of the West India Company, were drawn to the synergies of the African slave traffic and Brazilian sugar production on both sides of the South Atlantic. The British, French, Dutch and Spanish sugar plantations in the Caribbean, all likewise worked by slave labor from Africa, were about to end the sweet times for Brazil's northeastern landowners, but nobody knew this yet. The Dutch landed in Bahia in 1624 and occupied Salvador, but they were driven out after a year. Five years later they took Olinda in Pernambuco and started a seven-year war that left them in control of the whole coast of Brazil's Northeast from Fortaleza in Ceará to the São Francisco River South of Alagoas.

For seven years the Dutch ruled most of the Northeast from Recife. They were enlightened rulers, compared with the Portuguese. Dreaming of Amsterdam, Prince Maurits of Nassau built Recife's canals, brought out scientists and painters to record the wonders of the New World in the tropics, encouraged Amsterdam's Jewish business community to emigrate. He founded synagogues in Recife while the Inquisition was trying to exterminate Judaism on the continent. In Africa, Nassau seized Portugal's slave trading entrepôts on the coast of the Gulf of Guinea and Angola. The big Portuguese landowners of Pernambuco fought back from the interior with a guerrilla resistance and the Dutch were forced back on Recife. By midcentury, the Dutch had their new war with England to constrain them and the West India Company was in deep financial trouble. In 1654 the Protestant invaders withdrew altogether. The costs for the colonial powers had been nearly ruinous on both sides.

For the African slaves of Pernambuco the disturbances of the

Dutch grab for the Northeast were an opportunity they seized. A lot of fugitives had already been gathering in a forested and hilly inland area to the south, a range running parallel to the coast between Recife and Maceió, about seventy kilometers inland. It was called Palmares after the forests of wild palms that were dense in those hills—palms which afforded the fugitives *wine, oil, salt and clothing . . . their leaves serve as roofing, their branches for supports, the fruit for sustenance . . . and the fibre in the trunk makes string and rope.* A network of nine *quilombos*—an African word for a warrior brotherhood gave the settlements their name—grew up in the hills of Palmares, and by 1612 the *republic* was enough of a threat to the slave owners for an armed expedition of six hundred men to be sent to destroy it.

All the expedition realized was the size of the difficulty. The rugged, trackless and densely forested hills were almost impenetrable and the quilombos were spread widely. Palmares went on growing while the Portuguese colonists fought the Dutch invaders. Not only African slaves settled there but índios and even whites who were in flight from the law or the Inquisition. The Dutch in their turn saw the quilombos as *a serious threat* in 1640. There were now six thousand people living in the capital, Macaco, a fortified town built on the Serra da Barriga, the highest ridge. The Dutch mounted a raid in 1644 and killed a hundred of them, and another the following year.

Ten years later, when the Portuguese regained control of the colony, Palmares was bigger than ever. A white man who had lived there told the Portuguese authorities the quilombos were armed with guns and bows and arrows for hunting and self-defense, the towns well fortified and their houses laid out in streets with chapels, statues and *palaces*. The people grew crops of corn, manioc, sweet potato, beans, bananas and sugarcane, raised chicken and pigs, ran foundries, workshops, potteries and carpentry shops. The índios taught the Africans pottery, fishing, hunting, netmaking. The Africans passed on the technology they had learned on the sugar estates. The women were relatively few, but their numbers were boosted by raids and they shared themselves around in a system of polyandry and before long there were many children in Palmares, as there never had been in the slave quarters. The children grew up. The settlement was more than a generation old. Its king had a wife and two young concubines; the other men made do.

For the colonists it was terrible news. The Africans and their allies were occupying the richest agricultural land—the valleys between the fortified hilltops were marvelous for grazing—and the next most accessible after the narrow coastal strip. The Portuguese seafarers had always been lazy and rather scared about penetrating the interior of the South American continent. Now the government was getting sterner. Settlers had to push inland. Cattle were being raised and cattle needed land. The fertile hills and valleys of Palmares were earmarked for Portuguese expansion and had to be cleared of rebels. The Portuguese were more rawly conscious than ever, at the almost accidental end of twenty years of Dutch occupation, that their own situation in Brazil was very precarious. Soon after the middle of the seventeenth century the population of Palmares reached twenty thousand. This made it, along with Salvador de Bahia and the Recife-Olinda settlement, one of the three biggest urban centers in Brazil. What if some other European power—France, England—wanted to move in after the Dutch? What if they did a deal with Palmares? Palmares also had a stable leadership and its leaders necessarily had a sharp understanding of political realities. The great leader of Palmares at this time was Ganga Zumba, the *great lord,* whose

name was partly African and partly Tupi and who lived in the
main settlement on the Serra da Barriga.

Palmares had to go. The first thing the Portuguese did on
regaining power in 1654 was to send another armed raiding
party against Palmares, since *these internal enemies were just as
harmful and more barbaric and dreadful than the {Dutch}*. They
sent expedition after expedition. All failed. In 1670 the government of Pernambuco, alarmed that the landowners were now
negotiating directly with Palmares, planned its total destruction. Every year there were military attacks on its fortified settlements. In 1676 the military razed a fortified town of two
thousand houses after a fierce two-hour battle. Nearly all the
inhabitants escaped and built a new and less accessible town in
thicker forest. This was the first appearance in war of Zumbi—
a Bantu name for a military and religious leader—who was
Ganga Zumba's young son-in-law. It was also a breakthrough
for the colonial forces. And later that year Ganga Zumba's
forces, retreating from a new expedition, torched one of their
largest quilombos, *a city* the Portuguese judged it from its
ashes. Ganga Zumba fell back on another quilombo of a thousand houses, but this was taken at the end of 1677 and several
of the leader's children and grandchildren were among the
prisoners. Another son and several African leaders were killed.
Ganga Zumba was wounded but escaped.

The governor of Pernambuco now sent an emissary who knew
the area to Palmares. The governor made an offer. The escapees
of Palmares had seen how vulnerable their free society was to
the force of the settler state. The governor would grant them
land for a settlement and the release of all the women and children taken as prisoners. Africans who had fled from slavery
would be returned to their owners. All who had been born in
Palmares would remain free under Ganga Zumba as their leader.

If the offer was rejected he would destroy Palmares entirely and kill all its tens of thousands of inhabitants.

On a Saturday afternoon in June 1678, settler society in Recife was startled to see a dozen black warrior *barbarians* enter the city. *They came naked, with their natural parts alone covered. Some wore their hair in braids, others wore false beards and moustaches, and others were shaved, and nothing more. All were husky and powerful, armed with bows and arrows.* Two of them were Ganga Zumba's sons—one of them, wounded, riding a horse—and ten were military leaders from Palmares and they were suing for peace. They prostrated themselves, *striking their palms in sign of surrender,* before the governor, who *ordered them dressed and adorned with yellow ribbons.* A mass was sung, the warriors were baptized and swore allegiance to the king of Portugal. They set off back to Palmares with a treaty document and the deed to a forest *where there was no lack of palm trees to provide them with food.* The barbarians were seen by Recife society as impressed by the sumptuousness of the church, the size of the crowd, the greatness of the governors and the *friendliness.* Everyone was mightily pleased. Slave owner property rights had been reaffirmed, and Palmares would no longer be a haven for escapees. In time, it would be almost a normal settlement.

Only Zumbi was not pleased, back in Palmares. Neither were the other quilombo leaders, who now made Zumbi king. The irreducibles repudiated the treaty. Nobody was going back into slavery. Overthrown, Ganga Zumba disappeared. Maybe he was killed by Zumbi and the new Palmares leadership—what happened on the Serra da Barriga was less well recorded than the public spectacles of Recife. The governor set about the promised extermination. A series of *bush captains* led locally raised armies against Palmares in 1679, 1680, 1682, 1683 and 1684. Every year they were driven back. The placid agricultural settlement of Ganga Zumba had been transformed under Zumbi's leadership into a society on permanent war footing, and Zumbi's Palmares was unbeatable.

In 1685 a man called Domingos Jorge Velho came to Pernambuco. He wanted the governor's authorization to enslave the índios of the interior. He was a *bandeirante*, a *flag bearer*, leader of one of the armed raiding parties who had been heading inland toward the north into unknown territory from the new settlement of São Paulo in the south. The bandeirantes were the first Europeans to penetrate the interior of Brazil in a search for slaves, gold, precious stones. They were private entrepreneurs who lived off the sale of the prisoners they took among the índios while they hoped for a big mineral strike. A small party would spend months or years up country and come back with thousands of índios in chains. In the fragile order of Brazil the bandeirantes, who were numerous, experienced and hard as nails, soon became a de facto army. It was natural, when Jorge Velho heard about Palmares, that he and the governor of Pernambuco should do a deal. After two years of raiding in the Northeast and a good harvest of indigenous people—all the more appreciated by Pernambuco's landowners in that sugar prices had fallen sharply while the cost of African slaves had soared—in 1687 the governor and the bandeirantes agreed on an expedition against Palmares. The deal was payment in kind. Domingos Jorge Velho would destroy the quilombo and take most of the prisoners for himself as spoils of war. He took some time to deliver. It wasn't until six years later that he had a siege in place around the quilombo on the Serra da Barriga. The main quilombo of Palmares, the *royal stockade*, was surrounded by snares and protected by wattle and daub walls topped with iron spikes. It was known as Macaco—*Monkey* in Portuguese and how the settlers thought of it, though the name came more likely from a Bantu word, *mokoko*.

At the end of 1693 the bandeirante siege of Palmares began. In

February 1694 the redoubt fell after forty-two days. Two hundred fighters were killed when it was overrun and two hundred more threw themselves to their death over the cliffs. Five hundred prisoners were sold back into slavery outside Pernambuco. Zumbi himself and others escaped and fought on, and it took the bandeirantes another two years to hunt him down. On 20 November 1695, however, they took him, executed him and displayed his head on a spike for the edification of the African slaves of Pernambuco. After nearly a hundred years, Palmares was over.

The republic of Palmares had opposed a community of the oppressed, under African leadership, to the power of the Portuguese oligarchy. In the eighteenth century Brazil became more settled, and it was impossible ever again to defy the slave owners on the scale of Palmares, which had the size and permanence of an alternative state. Uprisings and revolts continued all around Brazil for the next two hundred years, and the communities of the fugitive were numberless. In 1835 the slaves—tempered by Islam—briefly commanded the city of Salvador de Bahia. The quilombos never again grew as big as Palmares, but around Brazil smaller settlements of escaped slaves, a few dozen or a few hundred people, were inextinguishable. The larger cities were ringed by them, like the favelas of today, and many of them lived, by necessity, off livestock theft and extortion. Most of the outer suburbs of Salvador today began as communities of escaped slaves. Quilombos perceived as dangers were suppressed by fire and slaughter. Others, smaller or more remote, were ignored and many lasted for a very long time. They outlasted the news that slavery was ended and are there, folded away into the remoter parts of the country, today.

Below the equator there is no sin. Nothing could have been better judged to attract enterprising male inhabitants of a Mediterra-

nean country under the screws of the Inquisition, or to empty
their minds of the fact that there were no quick and easy pick-
ings of any other kind in the newfound land of Brazil. All of
Portugal's overseas trade was conducted south of the equator in
the spice and textile trades with Africa and Asia, but these
offered their own rewards—for a shipload of black pepper, cin-
namon, ginger and cloves, the Lisbon market offered a twenty-
fold return on cost price—and there was no need to bring sex
into the equation. Brazil was different.

The *Holy Office* was not unaware of Brazil's erotic appeal. The
new city of Salvador had been going less than fifty years when
an inquisitorial *visitor* and his investigating committee arrived
in 1591, very seasick but determined to see how far the spiritual
life of the new colonies of Bahia and Pernambuco was falling
short of the rigorous new counterreformation standards lately
enforced in Europe. The interrogation records showed the Inquisition wanted to check specifically on backsliding by the *new
Christians* in Brazil. Portuguese Jews had converted under pressure at the time of the great expulsions from Spain and Portugal
and since the middle of the sixteenth century had been immi-
grating in large numbers to Brazil to escape the new persecu-
tions of the Holy Office. Now anyone who wore a clean shirt on
Saturday or refused to eat rabbit or octopus was under dire sus-
picion. The old Christians were also a great worry. This was the
time of the mass enslavement of the Tupi, to provide the colony's labor force and drive the labor-intensive sugar production.
The Tupi, though ready to sacrifice tribal enemies and prepared
to go to great lengths for the sake of metal technology and
weaponry, were proving refractory to mass enslavement and a
future as industrial forced labor. They had withdrawn from the
areas of coastal settlement, and the Portuguese slave traders were
having to press farther and farther into the forest to round up
new prisoners to enslave.

The whites were also having to enter into arrangements with the índio leaderships, mediated by *mamelucos,* sons of Portuguese fathers and Tupi mothers, already quite numerous, who moved between one culture and the other. Dealings were greatly complicated from an ideological point of view by the fact that the Tupi had developed a new religion since their disastrous encounter with Europeans, and it was a marvelous mirror image of the whites'. It was called the *Sanctity,* its leader was called the *pope* and he was backed by a pantheon of índio saints and a battalion of índio bishops. They prayed to a stone idol and exalted themselves smoking *holy grass.* They foretold the death of all whites or, failing that, their enslavement by índios. One of the inquisitor's first and most difficult cases concerned one of the colony's biggest landowners and slave dealers, who was sheltering the Sanctity on his land and was accused of revering their stone god when he went to deal with them. That the landowner had caused a pregnant African woman—from one of the first shipments of African slaves, who was eating dirt in her despair—to be thrown alive into a furnace was by comparison a venial offense. The landowner had only done it to frighten her and the other African slaves and was sorry.

After Judaism and the Tupi heresy, the inquisitor was determined to root out Protestantism and blasphemy and the idea that fornication was acceptable behavior, and anyone who had had contact with the French was particularly suspect. Sex being an ideological matter too, and the inquisitor having held out the promise of leniency for colonists who spontaneously made frank and full confessions, there was a rush to recount the details of sexual life. The rush was to get clear before sexual partners named names, and there was a certain studied vagueness on the part of those under interrogation about the identities and numbers of people with whom they'd had sex. Only a tenth of the

Inquisition records were ever published, but the first revelations from Bahia suggested that from the start the colony was the *theatre of vice* it was called by an observer a couple of hundred years later. One sin was reading the erotic novel *Diana,* which was on the index of forbidden books. Thereafter things got worse. The *unmentionable vice* was rife in the colony and the visitor found himself devoting a lot more attention to penetrations of *the rear passage* than to those of *the natural front passage,* though the activity of the male *dishonest member* was ubiquitous. There was a lot of sex between young boys and between young girls but also among married women as well as the usual suspects. First up to depose was a white bearded priest notorious for his activity among the local boys and for his passivity and *dishonest touchings.* Penetration or not? Ejaculation or not? the inquisitor always wanted to know, and whether the women had made use of a penetrating instrument. Some of the male penetrators were far too young—nine, ten—to have ejaculated, and others, clearly worried about the possible additional sinfulness of ejaculation following penetration, insisted they couldn't remember if they too had come as their partner most certainly had.

Married women wrote love notes to younger women and shot them longing provocative glances in the kitchen, older boys turned younger ones over in bed and mounted them, pubescent girls clutched and caressed each other nude. The inquisitor uncovered a relentlessly repeated scenario of lifted dresses, lowered breeches, creaking hammocks and movements from bed to bed under cover of darkness. Married women coupled passionately *like a man and a woman,* young brothers similarly. A man was charged with making love to a female donkey, and a herd boy on an island, perhaps lacking human companionship, *between the ages of eight and fourteen years . . . slept carnally, very often and in many different places at many different times, with many animals, sheep, donkeys, cows and mares . . . as if he had been an animal of the same kind.* Bahia was a riot of polymorphous perversity.

Distance makes it hard now to know what came out through ingenuousness, what through panic and what through a determination to conceal the greater by confessing the lesser crime. Was the woman who told on her husband for eating a slice of pineapple just before taking communion thinking only of the pineapple? People were right to take precautions, since the inquisitor followed up and cross-checked obsessively, especially the sexual charges, and other *confessions* were simply denunciations of personal enemies. The thirteen-year-old wife who claimed that her Greek husband only ever entered her by *the rear passage*—adding that he had *threatened to cut her tongue out with his knife* if she spoke—turned out to have been put up to it by her family, and the Greek was acquitted at his trial. The seventeen-year-old schoolboy who refused money for sex with his spiritual mentor changed his mind when the offer was doubled and promptly fucked the priest. Another man, recalling twelve years later the erotic crimes of his adolescence, evoked a pastoral glimpse in the memory of his sexual friendship with a boy who lived on the same street when they were both fifteen. Through the dire bureaucratic filter of the inquisitor's registrar he recorded that

in this way they alternately committed the said unmentionable sin, each one being sometimes agent and sometimes patient . . . very often, at different times and in different places, now at home, now in the forest, now on the river banks, and this friendship and this low relationship lasted for the space of more or less a year, with the said sodomitic couplings taking place thrice in three days, twice in two days, from week to week and sometimes twice a day, such that there is no way of recalling how many times said carnal coupling occurred, but they were many, as were many the times they joined their carnal natures and took their pleasure frontally, the said companion reaching ejaculation but the one confessing not stating that he himself did.

The other boy, he remarked, and whether with regret went unremarked by the scribe, was now married. The inquisitor was doubtless soon banging on his door. Yet like most of the illicit liaisons it had happened long ago and in the carefully given evidence the details slipped away. Endless frenzied couplings seemed to have been initiated by a young stranger passing through, sleeping overnight, gone the next day to another town, name long forgotten.

Yet in this fascicle of Inquisition reports of sexual crimes, there is no adultery, no simple fornication. For the church, this was a serious matter, so much that a score or so men were hauled before the visitor for defending fornication as no sin. Either the visitor tacitly realized his work would never end if he included simple male with female sex in his brief and put it at the bottom of the list, or else the inquisitors simply failed to impress on the colonists that even ordinary sex was a crime outside marriage.

The inquisitorial visitor spent four years, from 1591 to 1595, probing the illicit private life of the Brazilian colony. His sexual obsessions—How did the women copulate? How many times did the boys reach orgasm? Did anyone *see?*—and his minutely punitive preoccupation with rooting out Judaism and all traces of Judaic domestic culture punctiliously documented these hidden corners of life in Bahia and Pernambuco. Oddly, the Protestant heresy seemed less of a worry. The Tupi, who a few years earlier had flourished along these opulent coasts, had already been driven farther and farther back into the forest, and appeared in the records—which were skewed toward life in the more densely settled areas—only as occasional domestic slaves and already mainly present as mixed blood mamelucos, the first children of multiracial Brazil.

Gilberto Freyre said the early Portuguese settlers in Brazil fell into a kind of *sexual intoxication* as they had elsewhere, yet the sexual welter of Brazil was quite different from the distance and wariness of Portugal's erotic encounters with Africa and Asia. Beautiful and willing though the Tupi girls were, they were never the whole story. The sexual enthusiasms might have been spontaneous but at every point they were encouraged by the Portuguese authorities. Little underpeopled Portugal had to occupy coastal Brazil at almost any cost and start drawing on whatever riches its interior held. It had to populate Brazil or perish, and the Portuguese men threw themselves into the task with a will. They killed or enslaved the men and slept with the women and informal polygamy was the norm. Against natural inclination and the connivance of the secular powers, the church never had a chance. The church, moreover, as the inquisitorial records made clear by omission, had no interest at all in either the Tupi, the *blacks of the land,* or Africans, the *blacks of Guinea,* until they had been baptized. And in the face of the colony's sexual life, all the inquisitor could do was worry at the edges. The murder, rape and enslavement of the Tupi people by the church's flock found no reflection in the records of the Inquisition. What did concern the visitor, and very minutely, was whether a landowner or slave trafficker had bared his head before the stone idols of the índio Sanctity while he was up-country, or smoked índio tobacco, and whether the slaving parties when they were off raiding in the forests had eaten barbecued meat on Fridays or during Lent. It was not that a young Portuguese sailor raped a Tupi girl seen on a riverbank that disturbed the inquisitor, but that he had called out to his shipmates, as he leapt from the dinghy, that fornication was no sin. For the church, the local or imported blacks, unless and until they were baptized, were not entirely human.

The church had not got off to a good start in Brazil. The pope had appointed Brazil's first bishop forty years before the Inquisition arrived, and the bishop had found his flock hard to stomach. He was outraged when settlers took up the índio habit of smoking, and fought with the governor about the criminal license of life in Bahia. After five years of mounting indignation, in 1556 he set off back to Europe with a boatload of right thinking colonists to complain directly to the Portuguese king. They had barely left when their ship went aground in shallows just north of the São Francisco River and was wrecked. The bishop and the others waded ashore and were met by warriors of a tribe implacably hostile to the Portuguese invasion of their lands. In vain the sodden prelate's spiritual authority was explained to them by the other passengers. Brazil's first bishop had his skull ceremoniously split open and the warriors ate him, and proceeded to eat another hundred of Bahia's first citizens who had struggled ashore with the bishop onto what would later be the state of Alagoas.

————

On Friday nights Vavá's exuberance swelled with the crowds and the noise. I used to think it was his social nature taking off and fueled by the extra drinks he grabbed on the side as the work got more frenetic. But it was the thought of leaving it all behind that made him fizz. The Banguê closed early on Saturday and stayed rigorously barred all through Sunday. You would have thought Vavá was having the time of his life each Friday evening, and he was, but what made his spirits soar was neither our company nor the good business he was doing, nor even the extra drinks. It was getting out of there. Late on Friday night, when the last client—usually me—had tottered off, and the chairs and tables were stacked, the floor swept, kitchen cleaned, accounts done, the waiters paid and the last glass washed, Vavá vanished into the dark and he never reappeared until halfway through Monday. The secret of Vavá's elation was his house at the beach.

Sunday was always a problem. The Savoy did a good *salada de bacalhau* and the company there was always a hoot. The Bangüê almost never offered bacalhau, at most the odd *bolinha de bacalhau*. There is nothing better with beer than bolinhas de bacalhau—small balls of shredded salt cod mixed with potato, egg and garlic, deep-fried and eaten with squirts of fresh lime juice and pimenta—and you could make a meal of them. Coming from the North Sea, bacalhau was enormously expensive and the most insanely illogical of Brazil's imports, but so it was even in Portugal. Taste, as always, transcended logic.

Quite why salt cod from the North Sea became such a strong presence in the cooking of the Mediterranean seaboard I never understood, and still less why bacalhau—whose Mediterranean name seemed to be a scrambling of the Dutch—should have been even more popular in Portugal than in the coastal cities of Italy. Portugal had access to the fish of the Atlantic as well as the Mediterranean's. Yet Lisbon had shops selling nothing but bacalhau and offering about twenty different qualities and cuts. In Naples the shops sold salted anchovies and olives as well, and offered nowhere near Lisbon's variety of *baccalà*. Taking salt cod from the North Sea via the Mediterranean across the Atlantic and across the equator to Brazil was an even greater improbability, and the farther the bacalhau got from where it started the less cheap it became. As a preserved food it was just as resistant in the tropics—but who, living on the tropical South Atlantic, needed to preserve fish for more than a few days?

There was a parallel here. Australia's early colonial life and its insecurities, later but not unlike Brazil's, offered some clues. A genteel visitor to Sydney in the early nineteenth century was struck by never being served fresh fish or seafood, amid a plenty like Brazil's, only salt cod or smoked salmon. The meat was fresh, from her landowning hosts' own livestock, the fish never. Fresh meat was a landowner's luxury—convicts ate salt beef and hardtack or *xarque*—but anyone could throw a line into the waters of Port Jackson and take home a splendid fish dinner. Not to mention the oysters covering the rocks. The only way of asserting your social standing when it came to eating fish was to stick to expensive and inferior preserved fish shipped across the globe from home. I think it was the same in Brazil's Northeast. Whites liked to remind themselves they were Portuguese and fidalgo, and clung, after centuries, to the old ways. The common forms of meat in Pernambuco were dried xarque and carne do sol. Fresh beef or kid was costly and unusual. Fresh fish was everywhere, but bacalhau was imported and recherché enough to count as extracivilized, and far too expensive for most people to afford, especially the descendants of slaves. Discriminations in the kitchen matched the vaster ones in the streets.

On Mondays the rest of the world went back to work and normal life resumed. Vavá was never forthcoming about his other life. He brought back crayfish and pitù and fish wrapped in banana leaves, and I asked him where it was he went. *Porto de Galinhas,* he said. Porto de Galinhas was *Chicken Port,* and fifty kilometers south of Recife. It was where African slaves were landed in Pernambuco after British pressure had ended the trafficking in 1850. It was around this time that a phrase became current in Brazil about keeping up appearances and being politically correct. You did things *para inglês ver,* for the English to see. Through their bank loans and investments the English controlled Brazil's economy and had to be accommodated, and a show was put on out of respect for their human rights concerns. The prison ships now arrived clandestinely, with a nod and a wink and a leer and the necessary cash passing among captain and agent and the customs officials of the Brazilian Empire. Ships bringing slaves no longer docked in Recife. Shiploads of *chickens* were unloaded more discreetly down the coast at the *chicken port,* and when a new load of *chickens* arrived down the coast the landowners and people dealers in Recife knew what they would find. Business in the port of Recife was *para inglês ver.* Business at the *porto de galinhas* was business as usual. There was no real town in Porto de Galinhas, just a good beach with big natural pools in the rocks at low tide, and good fishing. And a random agglomeration of weekend houses kept by people from Recife.

When summer came, and I was back in Recife, the air in the streets was heavy with the fragrant smoke of festive herbs being burnt. The sky was a blinding blue day after day. No more murky turbulence of winter, not a trace of the inky clouds that had sometimes rolled in from the ocean. A permanent high pressure had settled over the Northeast. The air was at thirty, thirty-five, forty degrees. Inflation was running at twenty percent a month. At the Bangüê in the evenings Cândido dipped his cheese in pimenta and talked about the Northeast and the years he lived in Bahia. When Cândido had headed home with his bulging briefcase and his gently swaying gut, Lia finished the accounts and came over for a drink and a talk while Vavá worked. Vavá himself passed on pungent pieces of information about some of the unremarkable looking figures who came and went in the evenings. José plied me with questions about Italy. Sometime between Christmas and the New Year, Vavá inquired with a studied casualness whether I'd like to come down to Porto de Galinhas with him and Lia on New Year's Eve. Alexandre would be driving them down in the huge old Chevrolet. Vavá said it offhandedly, barking a few words out of the side of his mouth while seeming to scrutinize something on the far wall. I said I would, with a nonchalance to match his own. But I was conscious of having passed a threshold.

VI

Stuffed Goat

Lula later claimed that he and his friends *achieved in three years things that normally would have taken thirty in this country,* but in the late 1970s Brazilian workers were already starting to think hard about their situation. They had more than Lula's sprightly leaflets to stimulate them. The military had been riding the Brazilian boom for years and now it was dying under them and workers who had been eating started to go hungry. After a decade of no strikes at all, in May of 1978 the metalworkers in the Saab Scania truck assembly plant rejected the wage rise they were offered and stopped work. They wanted not only a pay raise but the right to deal directly with the company, and the idea of cutting out the government's union structure was the more dangerous demand. The strike spread to workers at Volkswagen, Ford, Mercedes-Benz, Chrysler, all the other big foreign owned car companies, and within ten days a hundred and fifty thousand workers were out. The military was caught wrong-footed. The workers got their raise and they got it directly from the carmakers. The striking workers were nearly as shocked as the army generals to see how strong they were.

The military responded by putting a decree through Congress

which outlawed strikes in *essential categories,* which included the metalworkers. In response Lula's union called a general strike for March 13 of the following year. The day came and Lula found himself that afternoon trying to speak to ninety thousand metalworkers in a football stadium that lacked a sound system or even a platform to speak from. There was only a little table, and Lula stood there, as he saw himself, *like a clown on top of the table.* His unamplified harangue was passed from mouth to mouth in Chinese whispers through the stands, rippling out in waves from the man on the table until it reached the farthest part of the stadium. *The strike may not be legal,* Lula said. *But it's just and legitimate . . . the laws were not made by us or by our representatives.* The meeting lasted four hours as tropical rain poured down. Two days later the government's labor court outlawed the strike. The day after that a hundred and seventy thousand metalworkers were on strike in São Paulo's industrial belt.

Everyone remembered the wet afternoon in the football stadium. *We realized that if we pooled our courage we became a giant,* said Lula. He had become a compelling speaker. *People listened to him for half an hour and thought he had been speaking for two minutes . . . they wanted more.* He worked from a few notes he'd scribbled on the back of his hand and he was drawing on something he'd absorbed as a child, maybe through his mother, on memories of the wandering preachers and ballad composing troubadors who worked the northeastern interior, men who knew their audience, knew their lives, knew how to transfix a crowd and make time stand still.

A week later, when the strikers refused to go back to work, troops of the military police surrounded the union offices and closed them down. Workers were banned from the stadium. Then Lula disappeared. There were days of alarm and disorientation among the metalworkers. Nobody knew where Lula was, or why he had vanished. Even later, it was never quite clear.

Without Lula, and menaced by armed troops, dogs and water cannons, the strike meetings dwindled. After days of panicky search the other strike leaders found Lula hiding out in a house, playing with his children on the floor. The army commander had telephoned and threatened to arrest him and he had lost his nerve. The other union leaders didn't know what to say. Lula didn't know what to say. The movement had got too big for him. But he got off the floor and went back to the striking workers. He went into the room where two thousand people were waiting to hear him and when he got to the head table he broke down and sobbed. People started cheering him, and it went on and on. *He recovered and made a wonderful speech. For the first time he aligned himself politically with the opposition. He'd never done that before.*

But the opposition, or at least the politicians who feebly opposed the military in the Brazilian Congress, did not return the support. Lula was in a weak position and got a poor deal and the strikers were badly let down. The workers felt betrayed and jeered their leaders, who wept. They were exhausted and badly scared. *Workers left the stadium that night calling me a traitor,* Lula remembered, and it was worse later when the employers broke the agreement and sacked the strike leaders in reprisal. Like the workers' gains, Lula's standing seemed lost forever after this defeat. But *he was born again out of the ashes.* Another strike was called in São Paulo six months later, but the military were ready and repression was swift. A union activist was shot dead outside a factory. Troops invaded churches which offered support—the Roman Catholic Church in São Paulo had an incomparably brave history of defending the people in the worst years of military rule—but something had started that was unstoppable. By the end of 1979 more than three million workers had gone on strike around the country. The Brazilian military had been in power for fifteen years. Enough was enough.

The restiveness among the industrial workers of São Paulo was always about living standards. For years the military had been cooking the books on inflation, and the earnings of Brazilian workers had been eaten away far more than the regime's economists revealed. But what made them so determined and so resilient in the car factories of São Paulo, after years of submission to the military, and what made workers all over the country act on their example, was something more. Their young leaders may have been groping for their tactics, but the people who filled the stadium were asserting their presence as working people, as producers of Brazil's wealth. Like the Polish workers in the shipyards of Gdansk who at the same time in another hemisphere were challenging a whole system of tyranny in demanding their rights, they wanted a voice in the running of their country. The São Paulo strikes of 1979 were about democracy. The regime's readiness to call out the troops against workers, and the failure of the regime's Congress to defend the workers' rights, led the young strike leaders ineluctably to see that union action on its own was not enough. Brazil's workers needed a voice in Congress.

The generals too saw in 1979 that Brazil was changing in ways that the military could no longer control. Military rule had begun its own long disintegration, which the military itself announced as *a process of slow and gradual opening.* It began with an amnesty for Brazil's political exiles who had fled arrest under the National Security Law. The politicians came back and started talking, the old hands, about forming a broad front against the military. Lula and the others found what they planned was far too broad, since it found room for some of the regime's old allies, people who were no friends of the workers. They were not going to play the old game. There was no going back now and in February of 1980 the Workers' Party came into being.

It might not have been a broad front, but it was a mixed

enough bag. At the core of the Workers' Party were Brazilians tough enough to have lived through terrible things and young enough to respond to the changes they were living through now. Compared with some of them, Lula was untested. One of them was a student leader who had been imprisoned early by the military. When the American ambassador was kidnapped in 1969 he was one of the prisoners freed in exchange and was flown to Cuba. There José Dirceu had his face altered and trained in guerrilla warfare techniques, ready to take up the armed struggle in Brazil. He was back in Brazil and organizing resistance when the amnesty meant he had to have himself made recognizable again. Others had already taken up the armed struggle. In the tragic wake of Che Guevara, another student leader, José Genoino, who was the northeasterner son of peasants from Ceará and knew life in the other Brazil, had been one of a few dozen creators of a guerrilla *foco* in the Amazon jungle. They were destroyed by a military offensive of fifteen thousand troops and Genoino, almost the only survivor, was tortured and imprisoned until the time of the amnesty.

The union struggle gathered new life after the near defeat of the year before. A hundred and forty thousand metal workers stopped work at the beginning of April. The government's labor court pronounced the new strike led by Lula illegal. The army and the military police came out again. A hundred thousand workers, with their women and children, who were gathered in the football stadium, saw the army helicopters hover overhead. The helicopters' doors were open and the people below could see the soldiers' machine guns raked above the crowd. The din of the rotors drowned the speakers' voices; the crowd stayed still and sang the Brazilian anthem against the noise. Lula and the other union leaders were arrested days later under the National Security Law, and held incommunicado by the torturers and killers of the Department of Political and Social Order. The strike went on without them and after a month they were freed. At his later trial Lula was sentenced by a military court to three and a half years in prison, but Brazilian justice was slow and by the end of 1981 things were moving irresistibly against the military's justice. The Workers' Party already had nearly half a million active members and by the end of the following year eight members of the federal Congress. Lula's trial was annulled.

The Workers' Party led the great campaign around Brazil in 1984 for DIRECT ELECTIONS NOW—this was the time the TV Globo news, showing the hundreds of thousands in São Paulo, claimed they were celebrating the city's anniversary. A million people massed in Rio to demand elections. When Congress voted against, the Workers' Party alone rejected the controlled congressional election of a new president allowed by the military in 1985. The following year the Workers' Party doubled its number of federal deputies to sixteen, and Lula won his seat in Congress with the biggest vote of any candidate in Brazil. In the local government elections of 1988 the Workers' Party won control of thirty-eight city administrations around Brazil, São Paulo's among them. The Workers' Party was unstoppable. The year after that was 1989, which would see the first direct election of a Brazilian president in twenty-nine years. In Lula the Workers' Party already had its candidate.

———

On New Year's Eve the Bangüê closed early for the usual reason—Vavá was leaving town—but first he had some regular customers to look after. A group of students always spent the last afternoon of the year at the Bangüê's outside tables, and while the rest of the city was visibly closing down and getting ready to party, this happy group stayed on and there was no way Vavá was going to hurry them off. I came back later and they were gone.

The Bangüê was closed and almost dark inside, but Lia and Vavá had made a clearing in the forest of stacked tables and chairs and were having a last cold beer. Alexandre brought the car around and we set off into the night for Porto de Galinhas.

Recife was not big on nocturnal illumination, even in the main streets, and we drove through a shadowy low-rise urban sprawl. We were making a detour because Vavá decided he wanted to drop in on a university professor he knew who had once bought a lot of wood sculptures. The professor was some kind of technocrat and a high adviser to the Brazilian government. *Part of the cúpula,* Vavá said. In Italy the *cupola* was the governing body of Cosa Nostra, but it seemed not to have a bad sense in Brazil. We got to a part of town where there were trees, and bumped along a narrow, deeply potholed street—the Chevrolet's suspension was almost gone, and you could see why—and stopped outside a pair of iron gates that made an opening in a high white wall. This was the professor's villa and ours was a surprise visit. We weren't out of the car before a couple of giant Doberman pinschers hurled themselves at the gate. In the dark they looked like small black racehorses with long pointy teeth. They seemed to want to tear our throats out. A barefoot youth in shorts appeared and grabbed their chains and wrestled them into a cyclone-wired compound beside the swimming pool. Silently, they hurled themselves toward us again and again and the cyclone wire pinged and hummed.

The Dobermans weren't the only dogs around. From inside the house came a frenzy of demented yapping by many dogs. The house was a curious stone construction that was part modernist and part Middle Eastern. Its blank outer wall made a second barrier against the world, and inside the rooms opened onto a courtyard with a garden of white river boulders and cactus. The courtyard was glassed in and made you wonder whether you were standing in a room or a garden. There were a number of large black wooden carvings from the northeastern interior against the walls and a dozen tiny champagne-colored poodles racing around and barking hysterically. The glass roof, the stone walls, the stone floor, the stone garden all multiplied the noise until it neared the pain threshold.

It took a while to summon the professor and his family, who were very much not celebrating the imminence of 1991. He was a stocky, guarded, hostile figure and his wife, who appeared through another door, was pale and hollow eyed and appeared to have been weeping. Eventually a young adult son and a young adult daughter emerged sluggishly from other rooms. The noise of the dogs did not abate and no one tried to quiet them. The poodles seemed to be trying to tell us something, as the Dobermans had outside. Vavá kept up a flow of bright conversation and everyone else kept up a pretense that human voices were audible over the barking. Since we didn't leave immediately— Vavá was irrepressible, and Lia kept her poise—after about twenty minutes someone sullenly handed me half a glass of warm beer. It was fairly clear that the professor had no plans to enlarge his collection of wooden statues. On our way out, I asked the barefoot youth if it was okay to pat the Dobermans. He looked at me as if I were mad. Happy New Year, everyone.

We headed south in silence for a while. On the outskirts of the low-rise sprawl, we passed strings of dark-skinned boys and girls walking along the shoulder of the narrow paved strip, on their way to parties. They were all dressed in white for the arrival of the New Year. The people wore white who sent off rafts of flowers and lighted candles into the sea toward Africa, for Yemanjá, the Yoruba mother of the seas. On New Year's morning the little boats of candles and flowers would be washed up with the bottles on the beach. All you could see in the dark night now was white clothes—white T-shirts, white shorts, white skirts, white shoes floated along in the darkness.

Porto de Galinhas seemed almost deserted, a darkened huddle of low houses on a network of dusty dirt tracks. Their owners were celebrating in town. We bumped along a rough track to a garden gate. A wide path with low steps led to a small darkened house at the top of a rise, but Vavá led us straight to a bower in a corner and set about lighting a fire. It was nearly midnight and time for dinner. Alexandre went up to the house in the dark and returned with a bleeding gash on his foot. He'd fallen, he said, and wandered off in the Chevrolet to find a doctor. But the charcoal on the barbecue was soon glowing, drinks were poured, and Vavá grilled some slices of zebu hump. Zebu were cattle from India—their name was Tibetan—who thrived in the Northeast, storing food for hard times in their hump, and whose meat was tender and delicious. At some point 1990 turned into 1991. We toasted. Alexandre came out of the shadows with his foot freshly bandaged. At some point we made our way up the path and tumbled into bed.

Vavá and Lia were up before me next morning and offered strong coffee and breadfruit. The house, Vavá muttered with more of his elaborate offhandedness, was just a prefabricated wooden thing like most of the other beach houses. The structure may have been prefabricated, but this house was not like the others. It was stripped back to its wooden essentials, which were all finely finished and coated with a uniform dark protective stain. It was like being in a nutshell. There were no false ceilings or wall linings in this hermit's retreat, hardly any furniture or fittings or any content at all, let alone random junk lying around. There was a restful austerity about it, a minimalism that spoke of a discreet but powerful creative will. Well ventilated, protected by a verandah at the front, across which a hammock was slung, a northeastern hammock with a lacy hand knotted fringe, and shaded by trees, it was dark and cool under the summer sun.

All this enhanced the shock to the eyes of stepping outside into the brilliant profusion of the garden. There was lawn on each side of the steps leading down from the verandah, and between the lawn and the high palisade of stained wood that ran around the perimeter was an opulence of flowering tropical vegetation. Vavá and Lia had brought each plant down from Recife, and made this garden. I could now see how carefully the shady bower had been created around the fireplace, which had a chimney to carry the smoke away, and the table where we'd been the night before. Across the path from the barbecue, under the opposite fence and framed by a brilliant purple bougainvillea, was a larger-than-life figure of a bearded Saint Francis carved in wood by a sculptor of the drylands. A garden hose kept water running through his cupped hands, and a flurry of small tropical birds were splashing and twittering there.

This was Vavá's retreat. Materially it was very little. Vavá and Lia had no money to speak of, and this beach house, hardly more than a cabin, was the only real estate they owned. In Recife they lived in a small rented apartment. A quality of mind, however, had been brought to bear on this place over the years. There was something old Brazilian, aboriginally Brazilian, about the austerity of the human habitation and the natural opulence of the simple well-tended garden. The índios would have been at home in this clean-swept space, the simple wood, the exuberant green. Vavá went on being offhand about it, but he was humming with pleasure at my admiration and my own pleasure in what he had made. This was a place of the mind, *Annihilating all that's made / To a green thought in a green shade.* When we walked down to the beach, calling on a couple of neighbors to wish them well for the new year, I saw how far Vavá's green shade was his own doing. The settlement of Porto de Galinhas was an arid, dusty, uncared-for slum. People had planted cottages on their blocks of wasteland and let the wasteland lie.

Rubbish lay in the dusty rutted tracks that ran between them. The green well-watered place surrounding Vavá's, and the look and setting of the house itself, were a single island among the dry and monochrome dereliction.

Down on the beach we met Paulo. He was a tall thin black man with big hooded eyes and was the source of the fish that Vavá had wrapped in banana leaves. He was the source of the fish Vavá grilled later that day and in general kept Vavá and Lia supplied at Porto de Galinhas. They had an arrangement. Vavá had invested in a *jangada* for Paulo to do his fishing from and Paulo, who had no other work, would supply fresh fish when Vavá and Lia came down with friends. We went out into the bay on Paulo's jangada and I dived into the clear water and struck off some distance, then floated and looked back at the handsome boat. It was a modern catamaran—jangadas were no longer made of logs lashed together—but it still had the beautiful uplifted triangular sail like an Arab dhow's that the Tupi called *cutinga,* the *white tongue.* Cabral's men had seen jangadas off the coast in 1500 and described them to the Portuguese king. Countless of them were still licking the waves of the Northeast's coastal waters.

We had a beer with Paulo on the beach, and from Vavá's sharp allusions I picked up a notion of Paulo's laid-back life in Porto de Galinhas, of the child he had fathered on a local primary-school teacher, a small daughter he took no responsibility for and in no way helped to raise but of whom he was nevertheless very fond and of whose infant exploits in music and arithmetic he was proud. Then Vavá asked after the *Swiss gentleman,* and I learned that Paulo had taken the Swiss gentleman, lately returned to his mountains, for an outing on the jangada and that the visitor had been greatly taken with Paulo. A little dalliance may or may not have ensued aboard the raft. Vavá clearly thought it had and Paulo didn't bother to contradict him.

The Swiss infatuation was well known around the water's edge and Paulo had clearly gained some cachet as an object of desire and maybe a little short term boost to his income.

Vavá talked a lot on the beach about the people we met and the people back in Recife. Cândido had a beach house nearby. I had never found out quite what the enigmatic Cândido did— was he some kind of economist? Vavá's eyes glittered. A relative working in one of the banks in Recife had yielded information. Cândido, said Vavá in a low voice, was the chief of military intelligence for the Northeast. We both had to remember not to let Cândido know we knew this. The news reminded me of the day I had been walking down one of Recife's main avenues by the river. A large American car had tooled past. The driver wore mirror shades and his elbow was resting on the door, and it was only when he gave a lazily economical salute as the car slid past that I had recognized Cândido. The memory of that odd moment, and the sense of being watched, came back now. But you never knew with Vavá. Back in Recife a few days later the chief prosecutor of the state of Minas Gerais dropped in for a drink with Vavá, who introduced me as a gold medal swimmer from the 1956 Olympics. *Goodness,* spluttered the chief prosecutor, slopping beer on his tie and shaking my hand. *What an honor.* I wondered how many other of the Bangüê's regulars knew what Cândido didn't know they knew about his work, and realized Vavá had been looking at my Italian papers while I swam.

If Roberto Marinho found something a little unreal in Fernando's announcement at the end of 1988 that he intended to be Brazil's next head of state, it might have been that Fernando— who had once modeled designer clothes at a charity do promoted by the wife of one of Brazil's dictator presidents—put him in mind of someone out of one or another of the Globo soaps.

Marinho had already noticed that Fernando adored the good things of life and tended to overdress in what he saw as a European manner; and he knew that Fernando's family belonged to that tiny number of Brazilians who might have found in the telenovelas' handling of dynastic conflict and family secrets among the very rich not an escape into fantasy but a kind of gritty realism.

Fernando was already better on TV than in real life. He had lost interest in being governor of Alagoas almost before he was elected. The results were barely in when he took off with Rosane for a two-month holiday in Europe. He came back in 1987 to a triumphant and carefully orchestrated landing in Alagoas. Bands played, flags waved, fireworks exploded and Fernando spoke from the back of a truck at Maceió airport. The crowd that had been ferried to the airport was dark skinned and short. Fernando was athletic, white and six feet tall, with longish black hair and a born-to-rule nose. He alone, in the stifling heat of that late summer afternoon in Maceió, wore a suit and tie. *All of us here,* he told his listeners, *are the children of hope.* The crowd went wild and film of that sunny afternoon was useful later, especially the aerial footage of the motorcade. The actual inauguration was washed out by a crushing tropical downpour.

He called them *my people.* The people of Alagoas were the poorest, state by state, in Brazil. They had the lowest literacy level, the shortest life expectancy and the highest infant mortality rate in the country. While Fernando was governor they stayed that way. Fernando did build the Virgin of the Poor Housing Estate on the outskirts of Maceió, which was still unpaid for when he resigned to contest the presidency, and a church dedicated to the same Virgin. She was his own invention, an image of the way he saw his people. Fernando was quick to pick up on popular resentments, and good on sound bites. He tapped into anger at corruption in the Brazilian bureaucracy, and since he had a vicious tongue when he was whipping up a crowd, his attacks on the president were much enjoyed. Fernando was young and modern. He was a *modernizer* and the visuals showed it. Suddenly, amid the dreary array of aging and compromised figures from the past, he was the second most admired politician in Brazil.

Early in the presidential year of 1989, Fernando had three very expensive television programs made about himself, each an hour long. He made deals with three small political parties which got the films transmitted free throughout Brazil as the electoral law guaranteed. Fernando and Rosane and the two children of his marriage to Lilibeth were seen heading up the Amazon in a small boat and looking concerned about ecology; Fernando was shown pointing at rice left rotting in government warehouses while the people went hungry. Fernando spoke vibrant lines against corruption in government and inflation of the currency, and each change of theme was punctuated by a chorus of young people shouting, *We want a new Brazil.* The first program took his approval rating from nine to fifteen percent, and the next two more than doubled that. By the middle of 1989, a few months before the vote, he was at forty percent and no one else came near him.

Now Roberto Marinho began to have second thoughts. He invited Fernando to the great mansion in Cosme Velho overlooking Rio. He and Lily had lately redecorated the whole house, and in the garden Marinho kept a flock of pink flamingos, flown in from Africa. He kept another flock of pink flamingos in the garden of his island home off Angra dos Reis, a beautiful cove on the coast an hour's drive south of Rio. Fernando looked down on Rio and the world at dusk as Marinho's pink flamingos performed their twilight dance, and he was deeply admiring of what he saw. He still nursed a secret rancor about Marinho's earlier dismissiveness but he didn't let that show, and Marinho was deeply appreciative of Fernando's awe at the Globo kitsch. *Brizola's been here half a dozen times,* Marinho said of the aging demagogue who was still Fernando's main rival. *Unlike you, he's never once remarked on the beauty of the view. A man who can't appreciate this view hasn't got the sensibility it takes to govern Brazil.* Roberto Marinho could not get his mind off the old demagogue who was in the lead, and hadn't noticed Lula's steady rise. He offered to fix things with any Brazilian TV channels that weren't already supporting Fernando for president. *Let me know who they are and I'll have a word with them.* Not everyone shared the new enthusiasm for Fernando. His hosts at one lunch thought Fernando was *clinically mad,* locked into his own fantasies and lacking all sense of the world around him. Some journalists noticed how brief his displays of youth and energy were at each campaign stop, how very short his *raucous and exalted* speeches, lacking range and tone. He scrambled back into the plane, slept through the flights, seemed gaga, never speaking with the press or his advisers, never reading. He looked like an actor, wrung out and empty. All these hardened political observers were remarking that a wider gap than usual lay between Fernando's words and the reality of him.

From September, a couple of months before the first vote, all the candidates got free TV time. Fernando and Lula each had ten minutes a day. The time was free but production values were not. PC made sure Fernando was constantly followed and filmed, and their campaign had $4 million worth of equipment, a hundred hours of footage already cataloged into forty themes and a six-thousand-square-meter TV studio. Their first effort opened with Fernando surveying Brazil from Monte Pascoal, the mountain overlooking the place of the Portuguese landing in 1500. His long black hair flapped in the wind. Then viewers saw Fernando defying the sugar growers under a tropical downpour, hair plastered to his scalp. It looked like a shampoo commercial. This was not necessarily a bad thing. Lula's hair was as dense and wiry as the outback scrub. But 1989 was not about hair, and Lula's team faced problems of a quite different order.

The Workers' Party had no money. Lula arrived to make his first campaign film wearing a borrowed suit too big for him. The studio was a rented room in São Paulo and the set was a desk against a beige wall. Lula looked around and asked, *Isn't all this going to cost too much?* There was also the problem of approach. In Brazil TV meant Globo and Globo meant soaps and managed news and the Fernando candidacy. Lula, some in the Workers' Party thought, needed a *people's TV* utterly unlike Globo's. The pragmatists replied that this would take years to evolve. There was an election to win and a style to use—the only style people knew. The conflict grew bitter. The conflict was resolved. Lula's first TV spot began with something strangely like Rede Globo's little logo symbol, the shining sphere that hypnotized Brazilians every night. The little translucent Globo ball came on bouncing and spinning until it froze in midscreen and people heard *Rede Globo, plim plim—Rede* was *Network.* This time the little sphere bounced, spun and froze firmly on the left. *Rede Povo, plim plim. Povo* was *People* and this was the People Network. Lula told viewers that *now they could see the truth on TV.* The Workers' Party program went on to parody all the Globo staples. *Globo Reporter* was answered by *Povo Reporter, Globo Gold* by *Povo Gold.*

Regime TV had never been laughed at before, not like this, on the medium itself. The Workers' Party shoestring shows led the ratings. Lula surged. TV Globo made plans to sue. Fernando, who was relaxing on a Caribbean beach when Lula's surge began, berated his team for not doing more of the gritty newsreel-style stuff that had produced his own spurt earlier. Lula's new jingle kept running through Fernando's head. *Lula la. Lula there.* Ooh la la. *A star was shining. Hope was growing.* It was insipid but infectious. That month Lula picked up in the streets. While Fernando lay on the beach with a forty-three percent rating, Lula worked the crowds. Sometimes, around Brazil, he spoke to seven meetings a day. In September fifty thousand people went for Lula in São Paulo, the biggest crowd yet. Sixty thousand in Belo Horizonte and there was a month to go until the vote. Brizola, the honey tongued old rabble-rouser, faded on TV. Lula, the week before the vote, drew crowds of a quarter of a million in Rio and São Paulo. Television, however, still had a part to play.

———

Lula pushed out Brizola. They were both well behind Fernando and there was almost nothing between them, but Lula came in second in November and now the race was between Fernando and Lula for December. The left had been divided. If you put Lula's vote and Brizola's together, there was a clear edge over Fernando. Nobody could feel confident. Fernando lunched with Roberto Marinho a week after the vote in Lily's Copacabana apartment, and the Globo patriarch came out after coffee talking happily about *modernization.* Elsewhere it was panic time. Fernando saw that Lula scared some people and that he had four weeks to work on that fear. In São Paulo, the head of the industrialists' organization announced that *eight hundred thousand businessmen would leave Brazil if Lula won,* and this was a good start. Fernando told the nation that the Workers' Party was heading for *a blood bath* in Brazil, which raised anxiety levels. But he was floundering until a society friend of his mother's told Dona Leda that her servants were threatening to occupy her apartment *when Lula won.* Fernando told a TV talk show that Lula would confiscate people's life savings. That families would have *their front doors broken down* and rooms seized to house the homeless. *You'll have Workers' Party militants living with you,* Fernando said, staring into the camera lens, his shirt drenched with sweat.

Lula went on closing the gap. Five days before the final vote, one poll showed Fernando four points ahead of Lula. Another had him only one point ahead, and the Workers' Party was famous for its dazzling electoral finishes. The artists from TV Globo did a TV program for the Workers' Party and sang *Lula la,* while *O Globo* printed a front page editorial on Lula called THE ROAD TO FASCISM. Fernando's elder brother Leopoldo, lately sacked from TV Globo and now Fernando's campaign manager in São Paulo, gave twenty-four thousand dollars in an envelope to Lula's old girlfriend, who went on TV and said *I could never support a man who tried to destroy my life.* She said Lula had tried to force her to abort their child. Lula was shaken by this. *O Globo* printed a front page editorial on THE RIGHT TO KNOW. There was going to be a TV debate just before the vote and TV Globo urged Fernando to look more human—less cold, less hard, less impeccable, less like a model, less like an automaton, less like *a man without a past.* Lula had done better in an earlier confrontation because he seemed like a real man with something to say. Fernando should *look as if he hasn't been resting all day. And not talk so much.* Fernando lay on his bed and stared at the ceiling all day before the encounter. He canceled his appointments and took no calls. Everything was slipping away from him; the whole manic drive for power had been in vain. He felt drained and limp. He had played the statesman and lost the first debate. This time he would act like a real person and go for the jugular.

Four hundred thousand people rallied for Lula in the center of Rio. It was his last meeting before the vote. That night Lula went back to São Paulo for a dinner with his unionists and metalworkers and it was daybreak when he got to bed. The morning before the debate he flew to Brasilia to meet Brazilian bishops and in the afternoon he flew back to São Paulo. He was exhausted, and went home to his wife, Marisa, and his children.

She was still fizzing with rage at the former girlfriend. An army of people was tramping through their little living room. While a barber trimmed his hair and beard, Lula said suddenly, *Tell them I'm not going.* Nobody took any notice. When he got to the TV studio, he said, *They messed with my daughter. They messed with my family.* The debate was about to start and Lula said, *I'm not going to shake that son of a bitch's hand.* Fernando smiled, suddenly energized. *Who wants to shake the hand of that scum?* Lula hoped aloud that it wouldn't last too long.

It lasted nearly three hours and seemed longer. Fernando ranted about *armed struggle* and *chaos* and *life savings* being seized and *apartments requisitioned.* Hunched and defensive and mumbling and standing on a box behind the lectern to bring him nearer Fernando's height, Lula inertly recited the Workers' Party positions. Fernando, who had earlier attacked Brazil's *corrupt elite* in the name of *the little man,* now stood against *rubbish, chaos, intolerance, intransigence, totalitarianism, the red flag.* The drab and useless old Brazilian standoff between wealth and labor, privilege and deprivation was acted out again, and thoughtful Brazilians were mortified. They were watching the past, and the country needed something new. When they turned off the cameras Lula said, *We're fucked. We've lost the election.* Fernando felt he'd won a resounding triumph and sulked for days when others demurred. He stopped speaking to people and lay on his bed and stared at the ceiling again and took no calls. There was a day and a half to go before the vote.

Roberto Marinho saw the six-minute Globo news report on the debate at lunchtime next day and he was not happy with what he saw. He wanted Lula more clearly the loser. A new version was ready for the Globo evening news. It gave Fernando most of the time, and intercut his more lucid statements with Lula's worst moments of stumbling uncertainty. The editor who made the final cut said, *I never did dirtier work in my life.* On voting day the TV news had something different. The owner of a supermarket chain had been kidnapped for ransom. On polling day police took the kidnappers, tortured them and paraded them to the media in Workers' Party T-shirts. Fernando's brother Leopoldo had been calling TV Globo all day demanding they say the Workers' Party was behind the kidnapping, *because Collor's election depends on it.* The kidnappers were not even Brazilian.

Fernando got thirty-five million votes and Lula thirty-one million. The president-elect came out of his sulk. A few days later he said to PC, *Without you, I wouldn't even have made it to the second round.* PC was over the moon. All through the year he had dined unremarked in the finest restaurants and chewed the bitter crust of the éminence grise. PC was too irrepressible to make a good éminence grise, and if he hadn't been such a positive person he might have resented the way he was always being pushed offstage as if he were some kind of embarrassment. He had been telling people all year how close he was to the candidate. Now, during the day, he called himself *the president's best friend.* Sometimes, after a few bottles of French champagne in the evening, he said, *I give Fernando his orders.* This got into the papers and Fernando was ropable. For the first and last time he threatened to break with PC. But PC needed people to know how close he was to Fernando. After the election, PC ran into a senator called Fernando Henrique Cardoso as they both left the Trianon restaurant after long lunches at separate tables, and PC told him, *The president likes you.* The senator wondered who the fat little bald guy was. This was the cross PC had to bear, while Fernando was already taking on the hieratic distance of a statesman. Fernando had his hair freshly trimmed in a more conventional, older style, and was already more formal in his dress and manner, even to his intimates. *I want to bring back dignity to Brazil,* he told them, his sense of himself returning as the votes came in. Brazil was now formally embodied in the person of

Fernando. And Roberto Marinho stood in the garden with Lily and gazed at his African flamingos moving in the dusk. Never had the pinkness of their twilight dance looked lovelier. Never had the view inspired such inner peace. Marinho was looking forward to his eighty-fifth year.

————

The northeastern drylands have a great population of goats. They are larger than billygoats and none of them is merely white. They come in brown, black, gray, coffee, dappled, piebald, skewbald. They have large, contemplative yellow eyes—quintessentially ruminant eyes—and huge floppy ears, which frame their narrow faces like great flaps of ornamental dark velvet as they stare in curiosity if they meet you on foot. They always know you are an outsider. A goat is a *bode*. Nourished by all the spiky, tough and fragrant drought resisting bushes of the dryland scrub, the bode's flesh is strong tasting. People in the drylands barbecue and eat great strips of it when they can, and when the best parts have been eaten, the entrails are chopped up and stuffed into the animal's stomach, an instance of the culinary resourcefulness of people who can afford to waste nothing. The *buchada de bode* is a dish analogous to the Scottish haggis, only much more interesting, and you never find it outside the drylands where the goats live.

I went to Garanhuns in the interior of Pernambuco looking for a place where the buchada, someone told me, was exceptional. I trudged around for some time before discovering that the place was out of town and next to an army barracks. The proximity of the army barracks was a hopeful sign and I found the place catering to poor boy conscripts and unbelievably cheap. It was barely noon when I arrived. Garanhuns is high above the sea and prides itself on a temperate climate, but I quickly finished a bottle of cold beer and ordered another. A young soldier was eating barbecued goat off a hot plate fired by an oil flame. Eating a lot of barbecued goat. Outside, other soldiers were heading back to the barracks across the square, and then a group of businessmen in white shirts and ties settled in and ordered the buchada. They had big soft waists and looked at home and clearly found the place worth a detour. A faintly ominous cloud of small houseflies and mosquitoes was hovering in the air. We were downhill from the town itself and, it was my impression, above a swamp. The flies kept landing on the rim of the beer glass, and later they dived into the plates. They seemed friendly enough.

Being a ruminant, the goat has two stomachs, and when you order a buchada you get a couple of small grayish bladders, the larger being like a little soccer ball with a distinct honeycomb pattern imprinted on the outside, presumably meaning the stomach has been turned inside out, and another smaller one like a tiny American football. They come with a certain amount of juice exuded from them, some poached vegetables, and the rice, beans and the *pirão,* a kind of heightened translucent gravy made by adding manioc flour to the juices, which no Brazilian dish involving juices ever comes without. The faintly obscene forms of the moist and grayish bladders on the plate, the grayish liquid gently oozing from them, the surgical look of the neatly sewn seams, the dubiously unidentifiable chopped up gray contents that spilled out in a little puff of unnameably flavored steam when you hacked the soft bags open suggested the work of some unmentionable surgeon. The cooking instructions, when I looked them up later, seemed to belong in a mortician's handbook. *Clean and wash well stomach, tripes and intestines . . . Add the boiled blood, which should now be solid, to the pan.* I have rarely tasted anything more delicious. Compared with buchada the haggis is a drab thing. Buchada, whose remote origin is in the inland Beira regions of Portugal, is fragrant with lime, cumin, black pepper, mint and coriander, as well as the tomato, capsicum, garlic and onions with which the chopped heart, lungs and liver are mixed. There is none of the suet and oatmeal that make the haggis the heavy and bulky food of people who live in a freezing rain-lashed place. Just a piece of bacon to enhance the flavor.

A very young woman served it. The proprietor was sitting outside in the big square by the barracks. His big black mustache flowing into a spadelike white beard made him look like Karl Marx in an old pair of football shorts, taking his leisure in a patriarchal way and watching some kids play football. The teams were largely made up of his own children. It wasn't clear whether the young woman serving was his daughter or his wife and it seemed indelicate to ask. In any case, there was hardly time. I had to meet Pedro, who was taking me to Varzea Comprida. I wanted to see where Lula came from.

This was the other reason I was in Garanhuns. Neither of us knew quite where we were headed. At this point Pedro had not even heard of Varzea Comprida and he was a local. But he had a vague idea where the clan lived and we headed out of town and downhill again, along a narrow paved road with scrubby plants on either side. We pulled up beside a middle-aged woman wearing a T-shirt printed with a faded Workers' Party slogan. She was striding along the side of the road, flinging out her legs in the tireless way of northeasterners, but she happily stopped and talked. Pedro asked her where Lula's people lived. Press-ganged into the quest, he was now as eager as I was. The woman was unsurprised, and spoke as if Lula hadn't gone south more than fifty years earlier, as if he were still out there in the scrub, and told us about a dirt track that led off the road some way ahead. We overshot it, but I saw an opening in the bushes and called out to Pedro, who braked sharply and reversed along the dirt verge. We swung off the narrow paved road onto a dirt track that we never would have found on our own.

We jolted along a narrow path over sandy soil, with a narrow ridge of green between the wheel tracks. The vegetation was neither dense nor high, but its pale and youthfully eager fronds leaned toward one another from each side of the track, at the height of a tall man. We were bumping along a dappled light green tunnel which from time to time opened out into a little clearing. We saw, at intervals, a goat, a sow, a string of hurrying earthbound little fowl which might have been quail. Once or twice a big lizard crossed the track, rearing up and throwing out its chest like a tiny angry dinosaur. In some of the larger clearings, behind a few large bushes and surrounded by carefully swept and beaten sandy ground, stood a little white-painted mud brick house, roofed with thatch or tiles. Near the houses were people, women and two young girls, moving along a net-work of smaller foot tracks even more closely hemmed in by leaves. These women and young girls were part of Lula's family. One woman, when we asked where Lula had been born, was starting to explain when Gilberto passed by. Gilberto was about Lula's age and size and had a neatly trimmed gray beard like Lula's, but instead of being covered by Lula's scrubby thatch of low-growing hair his head was a shining mahogany dome. Gil-berto was heading over in that direction and if we let him change first he would show the way. We followed him to another tiny white windowless house in another clearing of spotless beaten earth and he hurried into its darkness, scattering a family of small dark hens that were pecking at grains of corn. He reemerged in a fresh polo shirt and a clean pair of trousers and we set off along the track, following the plumy tail of an eager dog. At the point where we turned off onto yet another track that went up a low hill, we met yet another cousin of Lula's, a powerful youth in T-shirt and shorts who lived in a house near Lula's old place.

Everyone here seemed to be a cousin of Lula's, but there were degrees of cousinhood. Gilberto spoke with the authority of greater closeness. He was Lula's age, and the only one who looked like Lula. If Lula had stayed on the land, been fit and active and darkened by the sun, and not gone gray and soft and somewhat paunchy in decades of indoor dealings, he would have looked very much like Gilberto. And Gilberto spoke with a crisp and unassuming directness and a personal weight in his words that made you think of Lula. Gilberto was articulate and forthright, not overawed by his cousin, nor resentful as one left behind, and showed none of the babbling overexcitement of a city person who might claim some tenuous link to a celebrity. He was just pleased Lula had done some good for his people down south. The younger cousin, an amiable but silent youth, nodded emphatically. The family regarded Lula as an exponent of their own values and showed no surprise at his trajectory. They seemed to find it natural that their values had such a powerful voice in the land. It was not, in Brazil's history, natural at all.

Gilberto seemed amused by my visit, and said a journalist from Rio had been looking around a few weeks before. For Long Plain this was a lot of movement. Interest was clearly growing out there in the world. I asked if Lula—who was not formally in the running, though clearly the favorite by far—might win the presidency at the end of the year. Gilberto's eyes crinkled up. *He's already had three goes —*. I mentioned that Fernando Collor was back in public life and planning to lead Brazil again. Gilberto's eyes crinkled again. *You mean that guy who stole it?* We were wandering around as we spoke, passing an animal from time to time. There was one of everything except the chickens. A mule, a goat, a cow, a pig, a dog. Each animal had its own place, its own comforts gathered around it. The pig was particularly well tended, sprawled in a dirt bed under a four-poster canopy of dense fronds, trying to get some sleep in the heat, its head thrust into a gunnysack. Not for the first time, in seeking out someone's distant origin, I wondered why anyone would have wanted to leave. Varzea Comprida on this good day was like a pastoral dream, a magic world of people and animals and tiny white houses hidden in the green. Lula's mother had cooked on a woodstove and washed the family clothes in the river. But they had no food, only bought rice when the children were too sick to digest farofa. The children had no shoes. Even now, the little white houses seemed to have no electricity.

It's not there anymore, Gilberto said suddenly. *It was pulled down a while back.* There was a newer house nearby, where the younger cousin lived. The small buildings looked as though they were always being replaced and never in exactly the same place. A small rectangle of slightly thinner, paler grass, about big enough to park a small car on, was all that remained of the house where Lula was born. The air was thickening, black clouds had rolled along the river flat. A fine rain fell, getting heavier fast. We were miles from the road.

VII

A World Elsewhere

Before Fernando took office, in the first three months of 1990, PC set up in a couple of hotel suites in São Paulo, and there the industrialists of Brazil came to call on him. One suite was for meetings. In the next suite he kept his callers waiting. The waiting dramatized for PC's postulants just how much things had changed. Six months earlier, PC had kicked his heels outside their own offices and it wasn't until only Fernando remained between them and Lula that the business community had responded. Now PC told them Fernando's campaign had ended $30 million in the red. Nobody believed him. Since PC controlled access to the president and the government, he nevertheless pulled in another $30 million in what he happily called *the third round* of the presidential campaign.

In Brasilia PC worked out of two suites in adjacent buildings. One became the office of a company called EPC, set up in his own name, and this was where PC himself worked, protected by security guards and filtering the visitors he wanted to see through a series of remote-controlled anterooms. The second suite became the office of Salles Tourism. The office was perfectly anonymous. There was no sign outside, no name on the door, and no trace of a travel brochure within. It was even harder to reach than the first. You had to go in by a side door and down to the basement, where a security man checked you out and called the office. If your visit was approved, another security man took you up. Here the pilot Jorge Bandeira did business with people PC did not want to meet personally. The two suites housed the parallel government of the *new Brazil,* which was linked to the other through PC's Monday morning breakfasts with Fernando. It was the time of secret planning for the bank seizure. Fernando authorized PC to attend the planning meetings, but the economists hated him hanging around and moved their meetings to a secret place. Before the big freeze PC moved most of the $90 million to offshore bank accounts in the Caribbean. The rest stayed in the EPC accounts to pay the expenses of Fernando and his family. The week before the plan was announced, the EPC accounts were emptied too. Some of the money was converted to gold and dollars and the rest was used to buy up big blocks of land around Fernando's home.

Zelia knew she was unprepared to run Brazil's economy. As the freeze approached she began to lose her nerve. *Mr. President,* she said, *you realize a lot of people are going to suffer and even die because of our program . . . a lot of people won't even have money to eat.* Fernando impatiently told her to go ahead. Then Zelia fell in love with the new minister of justice, who was twenty years Zelia's senior and widely thought *incompetent and unreliable.* The legal provisions he drew up for the bank seizure had to be redone five times. During the long huddles of secret planning he brushed against Zelia's body and stared intently into her eyes. PC paid for the luxury chalet where the two spent their nights. The justice minister's wife, who had cancer, thought her husband was working around the clock on Brazil's economic crisis.

Fernando was sworn in as president of Brazil on March the fifteenth. The next day Brazilians with bank accounts found they
had no more than a little over a thousand dollars each. Zelia
explained on TV how the plan would work, and stumbled on
some fairly basic questions. She didn't know whether the money
seized would be adjusted for inflation when it was returned eighteen months later—inflation over the previous month alone had
been eighty-four percent. But the freeze did stop inflation at
first. Maybe, people felt for a while, the shock was needed. Then
two months later inflation was back at eight percent a month
and rising fast. Zelia no longer cared. She blamed the *inflationary
mentality* of Brazilians and flew away from their ruined lives for a
secret weekend assignation in New York with her lover. The
minister of justice had become such an embarrassment he had to
go. He wet his pants when Fernando's emissary required his res-
ignation and left by the ministry's back entrance. Then Zelia was
found taking money from the transport companies to let them
break the freeze and increase fares. A bureaucrat was brought in
to pick up the pieces. Looking back years later on the damage
done, Zelia's successor as minister remarked on the plan's

> great violence against the principles of an established legal order
> and the working rules of a market economy—unilateral break-
> ing of contractual obligations, freezing of financial assets, dis-
> regard of vested rights. [It] corroded the very idea of monetary
> restraint central to the plan's logic, . . . assaulted the holders of
> domestic private savings and so alienated a large part of the new
> middle class which had brought Collor victory at the polls.

What do you want, now we've won the election? PC asked Jorge
Bandeira. Bandeira wanted planes, and PC gave him five percent of Brazil Jet Air Taxi and made him its managing director. Brazil Jet had no capital and no planes as yet. The idea was

to start an air courier company. A second company, Mundial Air Taxi, was registered in Bandeira's name. Brazil Jet and Mundial operated out of their office in Brasilia and Bandeira took the calls for both. To get the money to get the planes they didn't have, PC and Bandeira sold prepaid air taxi rides to Brazil's big corporations. The planes were bought on installment plans in the United States—in two years, PC bought three executive jets and his own special plane, a Learjet 55 which was repainted in striking tones of dark gray on gray and called the Black Bat.

At the same time PC registered a company called Dupont Investments in the Virgin Islands. The sole function of Dupont Investments was to start another company on the United States mainland which PC called Miami Leasing. At first Miami Leasing didn't even have an address. It was fronted by a Brazilian who was living in Miami on false papers and being watched by the DEA and the FBI. The DEA was curious about the man's illegal dollar remits to Brazil, and thought he was running a cargo operation that carried cocaine. He was a light aircraft pilot and at the time he teamed up with PC he was also being investigated for trafficking in stolen aircraft parts and the illegal export of planes being used for drug drops. Under PC's patronage he became the director of a conglomerate consisting of Parts Express Corporation, Miami Leasing Aviation Company, Air Trading Inc., Interglobe Enterprise, Avtat Trading, Interglobal Trading, Nevada Trading, Pompano Jet and SCI Financière Albert Premier. Six of these had no address or telephone at all, and Miami Leasing operated out of the Brazilian's home in Miami. The last company on the list was registered in Paris and was the financial nerve center of PC's operation and its link with the Swiss banking system.

PC sent the dollars he made in Brazil off to Dupont Investments in the U.S. Virgin Islands. Dupont Investments sent the money on to Miami Leasing and Miami Leasing used it to buy planes. PC's Brazilian companies leased the planes from his U.S. companies and that way he got the planes into Brazil duty-free. The first was the Black Bat at the end of 1990. The second plane arrived with its papers so crudely forged that the plane's American dispatcher, who was already under DEA investigation for laundering money for the cocaine cartels, went down for some time. That was his problem, not PC's. The beauty of the arrangement was that PC could now send money regularly and legally to the United States as the fee owed to Miami Leasing on these two leasing contracts. He remitted $1.5 million from Brazil to the States every month.

While Brazil's largest real air taxi company was nose-diving into debt, Brasil Jet and Mundial made millions. Brasil Jet logged nearly five hundred flights with the Black Bat and Mundial recorded nearly four hundred with the other plane. In reality, the only person who flew in the Black Bat was PC himself, and the occasional special guest. PC made a quick trip in the Black Bat from Recife to Lisbon and Paris and back over a few days at the end of June in 1991, and that flight cost an imaginary client over half a million dollars. Another of Brasil Jet's biggest customers was OAS Construction, a real corporation which was winning more public works contracts from the Brazilian government than any other. Odebrecht Construction was a similarly big spender with Mundial, and the receipts for the millions it paid to Mundial bore the dates of public works contracts Odebrecht had signed with the Brazilian government. A lot of the real flights being logged by Bandeira in PC's planes were along the drug routes of the Americas, from Brazil to the United States, Venezuela, Bolivia, Cuba and Guyana. And in the first year of Fernando's presidency there were dozens of flights to Caribbean islands offering special offshore banking facilities. The Black Bat made twenty-one flights out of Brazil in this period. In April 1991 Fernando issued a presidential decree ending all federal police checks on the passengers and cargoes being carried by private aircraft. It was part of his drive to modernize the Brazilian private airline sector and make it internationally competitive. PC had already come to a more informal understanding with the customs officials at Brazil's major airports and none of his planes was ever inspected. Things ran especially smoothly out of São Paulo, where in 1990 one of PC's friends, who also represented Dupont Investments and Miami Leasing in Brazil, was made superintendent of the federal customs. It was not the only high government post PC filled with one of his people.

———

Rosane had no intention of being merely decorative as first lady. When she began to make her own way in the world, Globo's viewing public was bemused to find a new soap playing in the news slot. It might have been called *First Couple,* or *Rosane Takes Over.* It was immensely popular, and as in other soaps the content of each new episode was decided by audience ratings for the one just shown. Earlier in 1990 Rosane had concentrated on shopping. *Madame is spending a lot,* PC said with professional awe. He wondered about the solid gold Rolex, a man's model that nobody ever saw on the president's wrist, when he released the funds to buy it. Sometimes PC sighed, *Madame is spending too much.* The first family's personal expenses were far more than Fernando's income. In two and a half years PC paid out $6.5 million dollars to Fernando, and also financed his private secretary and his press secretary, who was running up credit card bills for double his salary and lighting his Havana cigars with hundred-dollar banknotes. PC transferred the money discreetly from several accounts in the name of several imaginary people in several different banks. Fernando's personal secretary used three different identities, holding three different accounts in three different banks to receive the money. Bandeira too invented another identity, who opened another account.

As first lady Rosane was president of the Legião Brasiliera de Assistência. The LBA was a government charity which spent a billion dollars a year. Its presidency had always been an honorary thing, but Rosane flew around Brazil visiting offices and projects and arriving home at night later than Fernando. Soon she was thinking of standing for Congress herself. Fernando was not pleased and made her promise to be home by seven-thirty every evening. She promised, but she hardly ever was. She was particularly active in Alagoas at election time. The October elections of 1990 for state governors, congressmen and senators was a busy time for Fernando and PC too, who wanted to build up a core of solidly indebted voting allies in Congress. PC raised and spent a lot of money and most of his people got up. The money came from Brazil's big carmakers, banks, contractors and credit card concession holders, and not a cent of it from the $90 million he already had. Again PC pulled in far more than he spent. In Alagoas, the two candidates for governor were both allies of Fernando. One had played an important part in projecting Fernando on the Brazilian scene and was the leader of his party in Congress. The other was a friend married to a cousin of Rosane's and backed by the whole Malta clan. PC spent $22 million on Rosane's cousin's husband, and maybe $1 million on Fernando's old ally. Rosane's cousin's husband won. Maybe PC wasted the money, since Alagoas hadn't changed all that much. An old colonel from one of the interior towns told a visitor up from the south, *None of this TV stuff works at election time. You just stick these country people on a truck and send them off to vote for the one you want.*

The loser assailed PC as *a gangster, an Al Capone dressed up as a public figure.* It was worse that Rosane, as the busy bee head of an enormous charity, had spent $11 million of public money in Alagoas in the month before the vote. Rosane had been to Canapi, Inhapi and Big Scrub, the three specks on the map of the interior where her family lived, and these towns got huge sums for dressmaking and goat breeding with no tenders called, all paid to firms belonging to people called Malta and largely imaginary companies. A firm of tanker trucks supposedly taking water to drought stricken towns was located at Malta Construction, whose workers had never seen a tanker truck. The registered address of the Pro Needy Association was an abandoned shed. No courses in dressmaking or goat breeding were held. Emergency food aid was used to elect Rosane's cousin's husband. Rosane had discovered a vocation.

During the year all this took to emerge, Fernando's and Rosane's relationship plunged into crisis. They were fighting about everything, including a magazine photo of Rosane in a bikini taken on a Maceió beach. Rosane gave a birthday lunch for her best friend at the charity—eighty guests, an orchestra, lobster and French champagne, and all paid out of charity funds. Rosane was taken to court. Three weeks later there was an ugly scene between Fernando and Rosane at a private dinner on their seventh wedding anniversary and they didn't speak for two weeks. One night Rosane came home late again, and Fernando hurled his wedding ring onto the bed. *Send your lawyer,* said Rosane. *You know I'm not afraid.* Fernando started coming home at midnight and they slept in the same room without speaking. *Why haven't you sent your lawyer?* she asked finally. *I'm going to tell my family.* The Maltas flew into Brasilia from their outback homes. There was a televised ceremony for the president's birthday, in front of family, ministers, governors, senators, judges, heads of church and diplomatic corps. Rosane went to shake

Fernando's hand. He turned away and left her arm outstretched in the air. It was on TV Globo that night and the pictures were everywhere. Everyone noticed that the president no longer wore his wedding ring.

Then Fernando heard Rosane was having an affair. He was white with fury and she responded in kind. *You believe this story? Just tell me. You believe this story?* Rosane shouted back. *I never believed the stories about you.* The young man, who worked on protocol for the Federal District government, was twenty-seven, well over six feet tall and known in Brasilia as *Handsome.* Someone had recorded Handsome's phone calls to the first lady and he had already left town, warned by the governor that *there were people out to get him.* Handsome avoided the airport, where his enemies were waiting, and left under cover by car and he stayed away from Brasilia until well after Fernando was gone for good.

A solemn mass in the cathedral of Brasilia marked the anniversary of the LBA, a few days after people heard about the $11 million of its funds Rosane had spent. Fernando stayed away, and while the choir sang Gounod's "Ave Maria," Rosane broke down and sobbed. A former first lady lent her a hankie to mop up and these pictures too were everywhere. It was the opening shot in Rosane's counterattack. The Maltas pumped out rumors about Fernando. *I'll be first lady until the end of the presidency,* Rosane said, *and if Fernando wants that to be tomorrow, he can go ahead.* She called a press conference and came with her father, brother, male cousins and an army of drylands heavies. Fernando had been known as *Ferdy Powder* in his student days and the big news at the press conference was apparently going to be that the president was now taking his cocaine through suppositories. *We'll see how macho he is,* Rosane said. Suddenly there was no more talk from Fernando of separation and divorce. Rosane's father had sent a message to the president that in the Malta family there were no divorcées. *A daughter of mine is single, married or a widow.* The Maltas owed a lot to their daughter, like the handsome new villa with a swimming pool where they now lived in Canapi. Rosane resigned from the LBA, and under the cameras Fernando kissed her and hugged her and they walked out hand in hand. Experienced viewers found it about as convincing as Rosane's tears in the cathedral. Fernando was resigned to his fate. He never wore his wedding ring again, however. The ring had disappeared.

One late afternoon in Rio, nineteen years after meeting the little march of bearded and bespectacled Workers' Party members and at almost exactly the same point on the Avenida Rio Branco, I saw another group of demonstrators marching stoically through the black exhaust smoke of the buses. They were different from the earlier knot of frail looking intellectuals—younger, more robust, darker skinned and more of them were women. There were some children marching too, and at least one young woman was marching with a baby at her breast. They carried a flag but no banners and I realized who they were. They were people of the Landless Movement and they were marching on the anniversary of a massacre. Five years before, nineteen unarmed members of the Landless Movement had been shot down by the military police on a country road at Eldorado dos Carajás in the northern state of Pará, south of the city of Belém. Fifty-one were badly wounded. The soldiers shot the farmworkers on the order of their two battalion majors, who were acting on the order of the military police colonel who was leading them, who gave the order to kill on the order of the state commander of military police, who was acting on the order of the state governor of

Pará, who gave the order to the military police commander on the order of a person or persons nobody ever got around to identifying with any precision.

The workers were not simply shot down as it were by panicky police. The police greatly outnumbered the landless. The police first surrounded the peasants and then fired from both sides of the road. Only some of the dead fell in that moment. Autopsies showed quite clearly—beyond the testimony of the people present, who were not taken much notice of—that most of the dead had been shot in the head or the back of the neck at point-blank range. And those who were shot in the back of the head had first been clubbed down and beaten to death—hacked to pieces—with scythes or knives. And a number of those who had been clubbed, hacked to pieces or shot in the back of the head were the leaders of the landless workers caught in the police cross fire. One of them was Oziel Pereira, who was seventeen years old. When the workers dispersed after being fired on, Oziel was handcuffed, led away by the military police, beaten more or less to death and then shot in the back of the head.

The people who were marching through Rio on the afternoon of 17 April 2001 were not simply commemorating the dead of 17 April 1996. People were marching all around Brazil that anniversary afternoon to mark the fact that none of the killers had been brought to justice. Charges had been laid, it was true, but the soldiers charged with murder were still on duty, and two sets of deeply flawed proceedings had been aborted. It was more than a year later, in 2002, that a third trial began of 120 soldiers, eleven sergeants, one captain, two majors and a colonel of the military police of Pará. After 120 hours of hearings many parties claimed were gravely compromised, the colonel and one of the majors were convicted. They were immediately released pending their appeal. Nobody was surprised. In fifteen years more than twelve hundred country workers had been murdered in Brazil, either by hired gunmen or the military police, and almost nobody had ever been brought to justice. It was an old story.

———

When slavery and empire ended, there was a spasm of denial in Rio's governing milieus of Brazil's brutal past and a sudden horror at the black and colored masses that four hundred years of slavery had left behind. The *scientific* literature of racism, which the theorists of the European empires were producing in such abundance at that time, thrived on these anxieties. Cranial measurements were all the rage among the intellectuals of a country that was trying to pull itself up by its racial bootstraps. Brazil—or at least Brazil's leaders—wanted to be like North Americans, like the British, like the Europeans. Brazil wanted to be modern.

The capital had to be made worthy of the nation, for a start. People were driven from the crowded center of Rio, their houses razed and replaced by avenues and squares, libraries and theaters, all copied from Paris and competing with Buenos Aires. The new Avenida Rio Branco was tens of times wider than the Rua do Ouvidor, once the smartest street in town. There was a campaign to suppress yellow fever and remove the tropical taint, the reminder of Africa, so that transatlantic shipping would include a call at Rio as well as temperate and European-seeming Buenos Aires, which was getting most of the immigrants and all of the overseas investment. There were mass vaccinations for smallpox. Most of this was window dressing. The modernizing *order and progress* was a matter of wishful thinking. Brazil got neither.

Landowners got nothing in return for losing their slave labor, but they quietly won a far greater prize. They had so finessed more than fifty years of political struggle over slavery that the question of land reform had remained entirely overlooked. Their labor force would now have to be recruited on the free market, in theory at least, but the vast landholdings were intact in the hands of the handful who had held them throughout the centuries of slavery. The million and a half newly freed slaves, without work, family, social connections, education, training, land—even a home—were left to make their own arrangements. This number of slaves in Brazil had stayed the same, through steady attrition and replacement, since the eighteenth century. What had changed was Brazil's growing number of free blacks and colored people. Even in 1870 these free dark people, all poor and unskilled, outnumbered whites. After abolition the whites were an even smaller minority, which enhanced the anxiety the white masters felt about securing Brazil's place in the civilized world. The poor immigrants from Europe, originally brought out merely as one more form of cheap labor, to replace the disappearing slaves, were now valued breeding material. Brazil's elite had convinced itself the new republic needed to *whiten* to survive. Immigrants poured in from Italy, Germany and Portugal, and they all poured into Brazil's Southeast. Nearly all of them went to São Paulo. There, Brazil did whiten, and the economic center of gravity moved south and stayed there.

Times got bad in the Northeast. In the early days of the southern coffee boom in the 1870s, the living standards of northeasterners had been much like the southeasterners'. But soon coffee was earning considerably more than everything else Brazil produced put together, while in the Northeast sugar and cotton, which had been earning half of Brazil's entire income in the 1820s, were ninety years later earning three percent. Growers were getting less for their sugar than they paid to get it to the ports and everywhere plantations were going bankrupt. Cacao and tobacco were doing no better. In the last decade of the nineteenth century the Southeast and the Northeast of Brazil became two different countries.

The Northeast was not a good place to be released from slavery into the free market. It was not a good time to be a person of mixed race at all, and the Northeast had four hundred years of mixing among índios, Portuguese and Africans behind it. No landowners in the flourishing Southeast wanted *dark, backward, lazy* Brazilian northeasterners on their payroll when they could get fresh, smart eager white labor from Europe. For an elite yearning for *gringo* efficiency and French style, the Northeast was now an embarrassment and a liability, with a dying economy and a bastard people. This was how people thought. The Northeast's cotton boom had come in the sixties and gone in the seventies, lasting no longer than North America's Civil War over slavery. It had lured many thousands to the interior in time for a terrible drought. The newest hope was the Amazon rain forest and its rubber plantations. Rubber was the very latest growth spurt in the endless history of Brazil's boom-and-bust commodity economy. The Amazon was a long way away and a rubber tapper's life was a new kind of slavery but hundreds of thousands made the journey from the northeastern drylands to try it.

Others stayed on the bleak dryland of the Northeast's interior, trying to do sharecropping on little land and less water. The land was utterly unsuited to agriculture and desperately unproductive, nearly exhausted by centuries of overgrazing and further depleted now by the slash-and-burn practices the new people brought from the coast. Half a million people of the interior died in the *great drought* that finally broke in 1879. It was followed by a worse one ten years later, just as slavery ended and yet more people were driven to scrabble a living from the stony waterless ground, and lasted four years. None of the Northeast's big landowners, having held on to their estates through the rocky days when the slaves were freed and the empire vanished, offered them anything.

The landowners of the interior were doing quite well, though less well than the planters on the coast. They controlled the water sources on the ground and were paid off in *drought relief* for supporting a state governor who had his ties to the prosperous government in Rio. The hungry landless people of the interior made a convenient pool of docile casual labor for the cattle stations. In 1889 the British consul in Recife reported to London that labor was cheaper in Pernambuco than anywhere in the world outside Asia. And the dire condition of the Northeast was starting to impinge on the rest of the country. Brazil's growth was slowing, in spite of coffee, in spite of rubber. The Northeast's second great drought broke briefly in 1890, but returned worse than ever the next year, and then the coffee boom broke and Brazil's currency started losing value fast.

The people of the interior were tough and persistent, and they had to be. Silent and uncomplaining, they got by on almost nothing from dry ground that yielded unimaginably little. *A person who has to die doesn't cry,* they said. Fewer than one person in a hundred owned any land at all. Only one in ten could read or write. Their troubles were manifold. The physical bleakness of their lives—the hunger, thirst, disease—was matched by social absences. Government sat in the pleasant and populous coastal cities and left the interior to the colonels. The church was no more present than the state—lacking other consolations, the people of the interior held hard to their religion, but rarely saw a priest. They had some resources of their own. The landowners' bands of armed enforcers faced *social bandits* who stole cattle and horses, raided transports and homesteads for food, guns and farm tools, held up tax offices, stole what gold and jewels they found, then lost themselves in the thorn scrub. The church's negligence was answered by the wandering penitents and mystics of the outback, whose relation to the doctrines and institutions of the established church went from fairly orthodox to wildly heretical. These preachers and penitents were hated by the absent church, which they undermined without particularly meaning to. People listened to the itinerants when there was no one else to listen to, glad to feel there might be some larger order and meaning in their lives, glad when births, marriages, deaths became more than knots in a string of personal disasters. Hallucinations born of hunger, isolation and the austere intensities of the environment made the people's religion fiercely penitential, its visions millenarian and sometimes wildly apocalyptic.

———

Antônio Vicente Mendes Maciel came from a line of drylands cattle drovers who had gone on to do quite well as smallholders, until they had been almost wiped out in a long blood feud with a family of powerful landowners. Antônio's father had made and lost some money keeping a general store. Antônio taught children on the homestead of a big estate and then he went through a bad marriage and bad times making out as a salesman working the outback routes, and living through another relationship that went wrong. His troubles made him one of the drylands' solitary penitents, given to long fasts and little sleep and living on charity. He rebuilt abandoned churches and cemeteries, and preached in the evenings in the small towns of the interior on the need for penitence and devotion. He knew how to hold a crowd and had a way of lowering his voice at crucial moments, so people leaned forward, not wanting to miss a word. In a little town in the middle of nowhere, two or three thousand people would appear to hear him speak when night fell, from a makeshift platform under a canopy of leafy branches. His listeners vanished back into the thorn scrub the moment he stopped. The church and some of its priests on the ground tried to silence him because he was not ordained. It was, as ever, a question of control.

He was dry as a stick, sleeping on the ground and sometimes near death from his fasting. His personality had been obliterated, but his energy and his seriousness and his compelling voice drew people to him. He was neither a fanatic nor an impostor, though people who never knew him later called him both. People came to him for advice about the problems in their family, their money difficulties, trouble with the law, all the unfairnesses of their daily lives. They called him Antônio Conselheiro, *Antônio the Counselor.* People like him had been wandering the back trails of Brazil since the seventeenth century, but the need was greater now of someone to listen and advise and soon he seemed to be the only one. The Counselor was on the road all through the great droughts of the seventies and eighties. He walked the trails in his sandals, dressed in a dark blue buttoned canvas tunic, with a staff in his hand and a broad brimmed hat against the searing sun. Over twenty years he visited dozens of towns around the interior of the Northeast—in Bahia, Ceará, Pernambuco, Alagoas, Sergipe. As times got harder, landowners and police shared the church's unease at the Counselor's growing crowds. The institutions of property, order and the spirit were already under stress. Landowners were wondering how they would get along without slaves, and how they would get along with the military republicans who had so abruptly replaced the emperor; the church was being disestablished by the atheistic military; police were no longer sure where their loyalties lay. The lines transmitting power between Rio and the states, and between the state capitals and the remote interior, were all, during the years

of the second great drought, tangled or broken. Financial instability and wild speculation down south made the uncertainty worse.

The Counselor's moral talk cut into the nervously shifting
allegiances. He had always been against slavery, and freed slaves
came to him now. He had defended the market women against
the new taxes that made them unable to set up at the local
markets. When riots followed in the market towns the Counselor
was blamed. Most dangerously to himself, he was against the
godless new republic—not that he had much idea of what it
meant, beyond taxes and irreligion. The taxes, he said, were
driving people back into slavery. Everything was secular now
and the Counselor hated that. Over the door of one of the first
churches he built, he had carved the words *God alone is great,*
which summed up his feelings about the earth's powerful. The
terrible drought, the scourge visited on the land, was an image
of the coming end, he said, and his listeners found that easy to
believe.

There had been trouble over the years. In 1876 the police
officer and the priest in a town of Bahia's northern drylands
were put in such agitation by his followers that the Counselor
had to cross the state border to avoid arrest. The area's biggest
landowner, the future Baron of Jeremoabo—the title a reward
for opening Bahia's first industrial sugar refinery—demanded
the Counselor be seized. The police chief of Bahia wrote to the
archbishop promising to do it. Everyone was worried about
instability. The charge laid against the Counselor when they
took him was that years earlier he had murdered his mother
and wife. The Counselor's mother was found to have died when
he was a small child and his former wife to be alive and well,
but not before the Counselor had been manacled, savagely
beaten by soldiers, paraded through Salvador in irons. *Christ
suffered worse,* he muttered when they finally let him go. The

archbishop sent out word from Salvador that priests were not to get involved with the Counselor. They were to go to the police if he gave trouble and were reminded never to let laymen like the Counselor preach. Most priests ignored the archbishop, who was a long way away, but several years later he wrote again, requiring them to take a stronger stand against the Counselor, and quite a few did. By 1890 the Counselor's peripatetic mission was getting harder and he stopped moving around. He settled on a couple of abandoned properties north of Salvador with a group of followers. They planted crops, raised goats and chickens, dug a well, built a church and the place prospered through the worst time of the drought. Then the Counselor himself moved on.

The archbishop tried and failed to get the Counselor locked up in a lunatic asylum as a *religious fanatic.* The government thought that was going too far, despite the archbishop's insistence that the Counselor was a *subversive* undermining state as well as church and *distracting the common people from doing their daily tasks.* But then the Counselor's opposition to the republican taxes which were crushing the outback people entangled him in a power struggle in newly post imperial Bahia. In 1893 the state government sent a police patrol to assassinate the Counselor on a back road. He had been protected by tough country men—*jagunços,* they were called in the Northeast, in a vaguely criminal sense—ever since his wrongful arrest fifteen years earlier, and several were killed when the police opened fire. The others fought back and the police fled behind their commanding officer.

Antônio the Counselor again decided to retreat from conflict, to an abandoned property in very remote territory whose title was held by the Baron of Jeremoabo's niece. Canudos was in a relatively fertile river valley. It had water, room, good soil, and a steep hill above it called Monte Favella which commanded all approaches. The Baron of Jeremoabo was enraged when the Counselor's squatters arrived. Wherever the Counselor went now he would have found a hostile landowner and his police chief, and an archbishop fanning the flames in Salvador. The trouble was the people who followed the Counselor. A few hundred arrived with him in Canudos in 1893, to build their wattle and daub homes on land bounded on three sides by a bend of the Vasa Barris River, to plant crops and raise goats and horses. About three thousand people *armed to the teeth* were still scratching a desultory living in the neighborhood of the ruined homestead, drinking cachaça and smoking tobacco and maconha in long clay pipes. Most of them joined the new community and a few months later nearly fifteen thousand people had settled there. A year after that the population of Canudos was thirty-five thousand, living in thousands of mud brick houses. In a year and a half Canudos had become the second biggest city in Bahia, which was bigger than France, and Brazil's second most populous state.

Canudos emptied surrounding towns—one lost its entire population of five thousand. Some people brought their herds, others brought money realized on the properties they left. Women from slave owning families, moved by piety, brought jewelery and family valuables. Most came with nothing. Many had been slaves five years earlier, and all were in such a desperate state that they were ready to try anything. They came to live off the land. Men driven to banditry now saw the chance of a settled and productive life, and the índios who still survived in the district gravitated to the security of Canudos. People even came from the coast, and Salvador was seven hundred kilometers of stony track and dirt road away. More women came than men and all were young, since neither men nor women in the Northeast lived much beyond the age of twenty-seven. As livings dried up and withered all around the Northeast, people were already migrating in a driven, random way. Uniquely, Antônio the Counselor offered hope and Canudos its physical location. Soon Canudos was a self-sustaining agricultural community surrounded by rural poverty and drought. The Counselor himself, who was now in his sixties, retired to meditate, and it was the others who built the town. It was a perfectly free community, if rather austere—the Counselor banned cachaça and was severe about informal sex—held together by a strong sense of shared values. When the Counselor came out to preach in the evening they gathered in thousands to hear his dour compelling talk about the true faith and their lost emperor, the vanished well-being of old Brazil, the ills of the republican present, the new enslavement of the people, the coming end.

People planted and harvested, tended the animals, built houses and stores, traded their produce with outsiders. Corn, beans, arrowroot, potatoes, squash, watermelons, cantaloupes and sugarcane were grown along the riverbank. There were even banana trees, which were almost unknown in the drylands, and manioc grew in the valleys. They dug wells, built water tanks, warehouses, a schoolhouse, an abattoir, churches and armories, even a small lockup they called *the dustbin,* and the Counselor started work on a big new Church of Good Jesus. Some worked elsewhere in the district and came home at night. The children all went to school for a monthly fee paid to the several teachers and the Counselor started two other schools in nearby towns. His self-effacing but charismatic presence held people rather apart from their surroundings, and so did some of his fixations. Not only cachaça was banned in Canudos: so was the paper money issued by the hated new republic, which the Counselor refused to recognize, and business was done rather cumbersomely through notes of exchange. When the settlement needed things from outside, like timber or guns, they traded goat hides. Like any local colonel, the Counselor made all the final decisions.

———

Vavá and I were talking and we got around to seafood. Vavá asked me if I'd like to eat some lobster. I said yes. Secretly nervous about the expense—my time in Recife was being prolonged on a tiny budget—I maintained an outward calm. Later it occurred to me that Vavá might have taken this imperturbability as indifference to cost, which raised the anxiety level as the evening approached. Lobsters were a luxury and were outside the Bangüê's usual parameters. *How many? One, two?* Vavá wanted to know, shouting over the Friday evening noise. *Depends on the size,* I shouted back guardedly. *One large or two small.* Vavá was going to get the lobsters over the weekend and I would dine on Monday. Vavá went on using the plural when he talked about the lobsters.

Monday came, and Vavá electrified the quiet evening drinks crowd when he came over waving a huge red newly boiled crayfish in each hand. This was stuff the Bangüê's clients only dreamt about. The crustaceans were great deepwater Southern Hemisphere crayfish, familiar from childhood summers at Cape Otway in Australia. They were not wretched little Mediterranean lobsters after all. Vavá was unfazed when I said one would be enough. It looked even more enormous when it was split open. It returned thus, not much later, as a *moqueca,* and the moqueca was very well done indeed. The red shells were now swimming in a brilliant yellow sauce. The other eyes around the room made an intermittent show of being directed elsewhere, or lowered over a drink. A hush fell over the Bangüê.

Eating the crayfish moqueca was almost as painful at the outset as it was delicious. I am an untidy eater at the best of times, and that Monday I was naturally not going to leave undiscovered pockets of sweet white flesh in the hidden crevices of the shell. Given that the only aids to cleanliness were a few tiny squares of paper, that the whole thing was dripping yellow juice, and that José was prowling up and down in his slippers and never more than a few feet away, his eyes fixed on the plate like a starving tomcat's, and that I had loosened up with a couple of caipirinhas beforehand, it will be understood that the spectacle was not edifying. Further sets of eyes were drilling into me from behind the green coconuts, through the open window, from swiveled heads on the path being beaten to the pissoir and from the ladder rising to the kitchen. At a certain moment, however, the intensity of the pleasure and the majesty of the self-gratification made all else recede. I felt no shame. I sucked and slurped and shoveled rice into the golden puddles. A day's swimming and your appetite is inexhaustible. At last I slumped back, replete, and José hustled the brilliant debris away as from the scene of an embarrassing accident. He was okay. In several ways José did quite well out of this evening. Nevertheless, the look in his eyes stayed with me. The price was bearable. Vavá was thrilled with the unaccustomed drama and asked when we could do it again. Slowly, slowly I turned the pinpoints of stunned eyes on him. In the depth of satiety something stirred. *Maybe next week,* I said.

Next week came. Vavá, sunny and relaxed as he always was on Mondays, came up and rather abruptly said, *Pitù.* I knew what he meant. The word was written across walls and bottle labels all over Recife and the picture on the label showed another red crustacean, sometimes a couple of stories high, waving its huge pincers. In reality the pitù turned out to be not much more than the length of a finger or two, and not much thicker. I heard they could grow to a couple of feet long, but I never saw one anything like that size, then or later. The carapace was paper thin, the flesh tight packed and sweet. The pitù, Vavá said, was not a fruit of the sea but of the coastal rivers, a kind of finer freshwater prawn—a yabbie or a marron—and out of respect for its more delicate flavor, tonight he had it little more than lightly poached for me in coconut milk, though still with its cheerful tinge of moqueca yellow.

The moqueca is African and its real home in Brazil is Bahia, but people eat fish and seafood done this way all over Brazil. Along the northeastern seaboard moquecas recurred in endless fine permutations which tended to be better the closer you were to Bahia. Recife was pretty close and the versions Vavá rang down from the Bangüê's attic kitchen were characteristically subtle. The moqueca's bright yellow color is ubiquitous in African Brazilian food. It comes from *dendê,* the palm oil used in Bahian cooking. In a row of bottles the oil may cover the chromatic reach of a deeply glowing red gold, from cloudy to crystalline, from pale orange to deep mahogany. The finest extra-virgin oil, the darkest and clearest juice of the first pressing, is *flor de dendê.* The colors are a distillation of the glowing red of the ripe fruit, each one the size of an olive, that cluster by their hundreds in huge spiked bunches under the fronds of the dendê palm. The dendê is not native to Brazil but another import from the west coast of Africa. I wondered who first thought of bringing it across the Atlantic, and why—given that the tree and its fruit were of interest to the black slaves rather than their white owners—and it turned out to be a more complicated and uncertain story than I'd imagined. The question was not just who brought the palm to Brazil but who started using its oil to cook with.

In Africa the dendê first meant wine. In the first years of the sixteenth century, at the time of the first landings in Brazil, various Portuguese explorers of the African coast wrote about the wine made from the sap of the dendê palm. They also mentioned the oil made from its fruit, but only as used by Africans to soften and protect the skin. Palm wine never caught on in Brazil and the first mention of dendê oil in African cooking was made nearly a hundred years later, by an Italian traveler and writer called Filippo Pigafetta, who in 1591 wrote a curious and partly fantastical book on the *kingdom of the Congo and surrounding lands* using information from a Portuguese explorer, which after describing how the Africans *oil their bodies* with the oil *made from the flesh of the fruit* added that palm oil was *excellent in food.* Câmara Cascudo, the author of the monumental *History of Food in Brazil* in several volumes, claims that before this there is no record of Africans cooking with palm oil throughout the fourteenth and fifteenth centuries, and that it was the Portuguese, makers and users of olive oil at home for many centuries, who saw and developed the uses of palm oil in Brazilian kitchens, and not the Africans at all. It would make sense that the Portuguese themselves, in this case, brought the dendê palm to Brazil. The academic authors of the even more monumental *Cambridge World History of Food* state flatly that food has been cooked in palm oil for three thousand years, but they don't mention West Africa as one of the places where dendê was used to prepare food.

These days in Brazil dendê palm oil is a major export from the Amazon region, but this cooking oil sold to Asia is an industrial product that has been deodorized of its sharp flavor, leached of its gorgeous color and fiercely clarified to a pale translucency. In the Northeast the dendê for local consumption is still turned out along the coastal Recôncavo of Bahia by ancient and laborious means. The huge spiky husks are broken up with sledgehammers and the hard red fruits laboriously prized free. The fruit is cooked in a huge boiler over a fire of dead husks, then crushed in a circular stone press by the strength of patient oxen treading in an endless circle like the oxen that once drove the cane crushers on the sugar estates. The oil is released by washing, and the oxen's reward is to eat the mash that remains. The fruit's hard kernel yields another oil that in the old days was greatly sought after as a hair softener and that the food industry now uses in margarine.

A moqueca starts simple and can be elaborated using more ingredients into a very baroque dish indeed. To make a moqueca in its elemental form you briefly marinate some pieces of a robust fish, or some crustaceans or shellfish in some fresh lime juice and chili, then add them to a partly cooked sauté of fine slices of onion, red and green peppers and seeded tomato flesh and sauté them a little more—in dendê of course, though modern cooks usually lighten up in part with olive oil. Then you add some coconut milk and heat until the liquid boils and largely evaporates. You sprinkle the dish with fresh coriander and take it to the table with plenty of farofa. You can make a moqueca of almost anything—using steamed meat instead of fish, or gently breaking some eggs into the sauté just before serving, so that they poach with yolks unbroken. A moqueca of oysters was once the most astounding sexual restorative I ever enjoyed, but since the experience was unique it can't be recommended as a general rule. I raced back the following evening for a further treatment, but the oysters on the second occasion were a different lot, much smaller and quite useless. Neither at that place, a tiny restaurant named for a Yoruba deity, nor anywhere else was I ever offered this dish again.

Was the use of African dendê palm oil in cooking developed by the Portuguese in Brazil and not by Africans in Africa? Gilberto Freyre insisted that the name of the moqueca, the dendê dish par excellence, was a mutation of the índio word *pokeka,* which meant a *bundle,* and that the original dish consisted of a fish bundled in banana leaves and cooked over hot stones—Vavá knew how to preserve fish by making a bundle like this and putting it in hot sand. Gilberto wrote that in Bahia and in Pernambuco the *pokeka was deliciously Africanized, or better, Brazilianized* by the African slave cooks working in the kitchens of the plantation owners' houses. This was another version of his favorite insight, that the most Brazilian things in Brazilian culture were a synthesis of indigenous, Portuguese and African elements, and like the Brazilian people itself, new and unique. The marginal history of dendê seemed to be making the point over again. The oil was not African, or not just African, it was Brazilian.

VIII

A Place to Die For

When the emperor was shoved off from the Rio docks in 1889, Machado de Assis was fifty years old and the most popular novelist in town. Born in Rio, he had practically never left the city and was also one of its most popular journalists, commentators and writers of stories for magazines. They were women's magazines for the most part. Brazil's busy new middle class had been accreting around the imperial court in Rio and the traffic of its port for a couple of generations. Now it was enjoying the boom of the new coffee economy and the fruits of its own speculations, and had time for the luxuries the boom brought with it. Men went to concerts, went to the theater, went to the opera—you could see your friends here, make a show, and keep a sexual assignation—but the reading public's private enclave was entirely female. The first place you looked for fiction in Rio was among the new season's hats and frocks and the corset advertisements of the luxury magazines.

The magazines themselves were quite something, forerunners of glossies like *Vogue*. There was the *Family Journal,* for which Machado had been writing until it folded at the end of 1878, and the *Season,* the even more luxurious magazine which took its place the following month and became his outlet for another decade. They were both printed in Europe on the latest presses and had full color fashion plates. Only the literary supplement, the part Machado wrote for, was put together in Brazil. The point of reference was Paris. Fashionable Rio deferred to Paris in almost everything, making only the odd exception for the British when quality manufacture or efficiency of operation really mattered, as it did for gabardine and railways. Elegance in Rio—sartorial, gastronomic, intellectual—always aspired to be French and it still does.

Machado de Assis was not born to the class of leisured consumers for whom his writing catered. His father had been a house painter and his mother a domestic servant. This was about as near the bottom of the social pyramid as you could get without actually being a slave. Rio society, with the emperor at its apex, cultivated its social distinctions with more anxious energy than was ever required in the European metropoles. But the child Machado was taken up by the family his mother worked for—the slack and accommodating households of the Brazilian gentry were always acquiring *agregados,* who were neither quite the servants nor quite the equals of the people they lived with, and who passed their days in an agony of ambiguity. Machado got some education and started young and quickly acquired—getting a break from his printer's apprenticeship and learning to meet the brisk demands of the new journalism and filling the daily and weekly spaces in its papers—a pleasingly fluid, flexible, accessible, conversational tone that flattered and never intimidated his lady readers. A hundred years later Machado would have been scripting telenovelas for Globo. Writing for the illustrated magazines, he developed a style that made it utterly painless to assimilate the things he had to say. He needed such a style. Lolling on hammocks, fanned by slaves, sipping their syrups and juices, the ladies of Rio were not about to have demands made of them.

Only Machado did make demands of them. It was imperceptible at first. He turned out shapely little stories, barely more than anecdotes, on love and marriage, sexual choice. "A Husband's Wiles," "To Marry or Not to Marry," "A Superior Man," "Which of the Two," "Neither One nor the Other" were some of the very early magazine stories. Sometimes the sexual interest lay nearer the surface, as in "Confessions of a Girl Widow." When the first episode of this story came out in the *Family Journal* in 1865, it was attacked in a newspaper for its shocking frankness about sexual behavior. Other readers wrote in to praise the frankness and defend women's rights. The whole thing was likely a plant by Machado himself, an astute publicity move by a young writer who was also drawing attention to the real problems his story raised.

Sex was inseparable from class. It was sexual behavior that caused the deepest anxieties about social class, because sex had a way of cutting across the flimsy social distinctions Brazil's new middle class was trying to erect and threatening to throw everything into chaos. Sex was also inseparable from race, and it was particularly hard for the new bourgeoisie to maintain its civilized standards in a country that was fast being populated by a people who were clearly the product of sexual unions that crossed the lines of color and class, particularly the brutal line that separated the slaves from the free. The sensuous climate and the obtrusive near nudity of the lower classes were constantly inviting you to shed your imported finery. Even a well born white woman might *fall*. The men were falling all the time. The ever present personnel of the service economy were always presenting new invitations to your gaze and touch. The universal susceptibility and the barriers raised to stop your acting on it by the stern rules of family led to nagging suspicions and a pervasive culture of sexual jealousy. It was all the more insidious when you had nothing else to think about.

Racial identification tags proliferated madly as the nineteenth century moved on and the European middle class struggled to keep on top of all of Brazil's permutations and combinations of indigenous, African and European, mixes that kept blurring the necessary distinction between Us and Them. In a delicate and allusive way for the most part, Machado's first stories touched on the realities of class and race that constrained sexual life, but never too much to disturb his readers by reminding them how fragile everything was, or to upset the advertisers of the luxury goods imported from Europe which those readers were buying. The havoc that sex could wreak was always there yet always on the outer edge of the fictional world of the ladies' magazines, which always seemed to have the word *family* worked into their masthead. You had to be really sharp to seize the odd glimpse of the bitterness and violence that underlay the world he wrote about. Nevertheless, these things were in Machado's stories.

After a good marriage and a decade or more of very hard work he was established as a figure in Rio's literary life, and had quite a following among his women readers. He had risen in society. The printer's boy who had published poems at fifteen and made the leap into journalism had since brought out three books of poetry and four novels and seen several plays produced, quite apart from the stream of articles and stories for the press, which were already being collected into books. Machado's was an eminently nineteenth-century career: a talent had found its chance in feeding the voracity of the new print media and then it had transcended its origins. Over the years Machado wrote for thirty-five different magazines and newspapers. In his career he was a later and Brazilian version of Dickens, of Balzac—a prodigy, a celebrity, a social success as much as a literary one. In a

Francophile, Latin and less rambunctious way, Machado was like his North American contemporary Mark Twain. The social dimension of his career through the 1870s had been as remarkable as his output. And Machado the unfalteringly productive writer had for thirteen years also been a fast rising public servant. He had even, much against his own inclination, stood for parliament.

In late 1878, when he was a few months shy of forty, Machado broke down. The medical reticence of the age and his own exceeding discretion meant that the nature of his collapse and what brought it on were never made clear. Had he been driving himself too hard? Balzac had barely survived to fifty. Dickens never reached sixty. In Rio the prognosis was worse, and any man facing a systemic breakdown at forty would have expected death. The *girl widows* of Machado's own stories were a reality that ignored class and race. The deceased had often worn a velvet tie and a black frockcoat and many of the widows sported big hats and bustles. Rio was an overcrowded unplanned European metropolis that had grown in a tropical climate without thought of sanitation or of what, in that latitude, the European models of urban life might mean. Malaria, dengue, cholera, syphilis, leprosy and yellow fever were endemic. *It is impossible to think of Rio de Janeiro in the nineteenth century without being haunted by this mortal spectre,* remarked Fernand Braudel of the yellow fever that had come from Africa with the slaves.

Machado left the busy round of his social and cultural activities, took leave from the ministry, suspended his magazine writing for six months—they would be the only six months in forty years that he was not producing material for several periodicals at a time. He left Rio and went with his wife, Carolina, to a small hill town for total rest. It was his first holiday, the first time they had been alone together. His eyes were giving him worse trouble than usual. He was almost blind, could neither read nor write, so Carolina read to him and took dictation. He had always had a stammer, and had been epileptic as a child. Was it an epileptic crisis? Before the collapse he had told a friend, *I'm heading for consumption of the small intestine with giant strides.* The diagnosis was curiously particular. There was no other indication that tuberculosis was his problem, and the highly clinical suggestiveness of his own account was perhaps intended to throw people off the track. He got over it. And not long after Machado went back to work in 1879 from his six months of social nonexistence, when he was still almost blind, he began dictating a new novel to his wife. Early the next year his disconcerted readers encountered the first fragmentary installments of *The Posthumous Memoirs of Bras Cubas* in their favorite magazine.

That they listened at all to this voice from the dead was its triumph. All Machado's art was in the laid-back, funny, disabused and hypnotically conversational tone of Bras—late *homme moyen sensuel* of the Brazilian ruling class, an underachiever even by the lights of that deeply relaxed milieu—speaking from beyond the grave about the events of an uneventful life. This was a great change from Machado's earlier novels and tales about disadvantaged young women struggling for romantic fulfillment and a place in society, a fulfillment they usually and reassuringly found. Bras Cubas took Machado's *pale lady readers* into the male mind. And from beyond the grave Bras is free to speak as frankly and as inconsequentially as he feels like doing, dwelling on tiny details when he likes and skipping what bores him, since *frankness is the prime virtue of a dead man.* Technically, Machado had found in Laurence Sterne's whimsical eighteenth-century protonovel *Tristram Shandy* a way of getting free of the relentlessly external procedures of the realistic novel, and he owed even more to the ruthlessly direct—even cruel and petty—truthtelling of Stendhal's personal writings. But the cruel realities were painlessly assimilated through Machado's lightly insinuating prose.

Seduced by the conversational tone, the lady readers found themselves encountering some unexpected realities—learning that the child Bras at the age of six had *split open the head of a slave because she'd refused to give me a spoonful of the coconut confection she was making.* And that he whipped a black houseboy of his own age, saying when the other child complained, *Shut your mouth, animal.* These glimpses of domestic life in the slave owning households of Brazil were ordinary enough—Gilberto Freyre would document them amply—but disconcerting to meet in a novel. Likewise, the long adultery with a politician's wife which comprises the central fact of Bras's life as a man. Adultery was still an electrifying subject for a novel's lady readers, but in *Bras Cubas* it is neither daring nor tragic nor even a cynical seduction. Bras and Virgilia live a purely sexual relationship which eventually fades from the very lack of obstacles it encounters, an adultery as dull in the end as a bourgeois marriage. Just as Bras's political career—the only career imaginable for a nineteenth-century Brazilian slave owner in Rio who already had more money than he could possibly need—dies from sheer lack of interest. Readers are spared the details.

Along the way, in this unexpectedly recognizable version of life in slave owning Rio, Machado's lady readers kept running into the realities of a woman's life in the capital, since the memoirs are basically the story of Bras's sex life. The child Bras spies on a grown-up adultery in the garden at his father's dinner party, his lubricious uncle hangs around the slave women in the laundry and later leads the adolescent Bras to the prostitute Marcela. The thread of Bras's life links vivid and complex glimpses of women: Marcela, grimly on the make and then obliterated by disease; the ship's captain's wife who dies at sea of consumption when Bras is packed off to study in Portugal; the beautiful lame girl he is briefly infatuated with; Virgilia, who marries ambition but sleeps with Bras; Dona Placida, the desperately poor and pious unmarried mother—seduced in a church—employed to keep the house where the affair is conducted; Sabina, his sister, who marries a rising businessman in the clandestine African slave traffic, whose slaves are thrashed bloody in his cellar; and the young girl Bras is being organized to marry when she suddenly dies of yellow fever. The men are all urbanely sketched nullities of conformity, greed, lust and madness.

The year *Bras Cubas* came out Machado reached the peak of civil service distinction as a cabinet officer advising his minister. From now on his career was a tremendous balancing act. The more truth he showed in his fiction about the higher levels of Rio society in the last decades of slavery and empire—and his intimacy with that world now gave him plenty of material—the more seductively he had to present it. To alienate his audience would be to lose everything. He went on upping the ante until his death, and although his loyal public grew increasingly bewildered, he never lost them. He became the ornament of Brazil's new metropolitan culture. The emperor conferred on him the Order of the Rose and he was the founding president of republican Brazil's new Academy of Letters, whose members wore elaborately frogged jackets and carried swords, in the manner of the Académie Française. Photographs show him transmogrifying from the long-haired dark-skinned sensuously open young artist into the angular close-cropped patriarch of letters, screened by the pince-nez firmly clamped in front of the failing eyes and made severe by its emphatic black ribbon, the abundant and now whitening mustaches combed ever more carefully over the still expressive and generous African lips.

In the papers and magazines of Rio, Machado de Assis spoke first to the European slave owners of Brazil, and then to the former slave owners, in the confidential tone of one of themselves, and he was valued above all for the worldly assurance and the relaxed elegance of language he brought to a Brazilian culture that had seemed locked into a permanent cringe. The end of slavery and end of empire were a time when Brazil's rulers wanted reassurance about their place in global civilization almost as much as they wanted to secure their place in global capitalism. Everything they consumed was being imported or imitated from Europe—of the time when he was alive Bras most fondly recalls the delicacies of M. Prudhon, formerly in the service of the cream of the French aristocracy and latterly *the chef at the Hotel Pharoux . . . He was famous . . . arrived in Rio along with the polka . . . the polka, M. Prudhon, the Tivoli, the foreigners' ball, the Casino, there you have some of the best memories of that time.* The English, who controlled the economy and had forced the end of slavery, lacked this charm. Bras's second prospective father-in-law tells him on their first meeting that *the English could go to hell! Things would never be right until they all sailed away.* In Brazil the English disapproved of everything they saw except the business opportunities.

————

Meanwhile, far from Rio and its indulgences, Canudos flourished, and as it grew it drained other settlements of people, drove the surrounding district's small town commerce even deeper into crisis and emptied churches of their flocks. More ominously, the Baron of Jeremoabo and the other landowners in a now depopulated region found themselves without that reservoir of cheap and pliant labor they had come to rely on. The people of Canudos had better things to do. The baron had always found the Counselor a pest. As the conflict over new taxes flared all around the interior into public burnings of the government's decrees, the baron saw the Counselor as a political enemy and a threat to his own well-being. It did not help the Counselor that he refused to recognize the republic at all. In the press and the state parliament in Salvador, Jeremoabo and the other colonels demanded that the state act against the Counselor, who was *either insane or criminal* and had a *sickening* ascendancy over his followers. Choosing the words most likely to disturb insecure new republicans, they said the Counselor was acting like an *absolute monarch* and forming a standing army of *criminals and fugitives* and *índios armed with bows and arrows*. That the last of the region's Kiriri índios had joined the settlement and celebrated their own rites there alongside the Counselor's Christians made Canudos even more the enemy of the new Brazil. The pressure to intervene against a settlement that challenged church and state came to a head at the end of 1896, when a shipment of wood for the new church at Canudos was confiscated at a port on the São Francisco River a hundred kilometers away.

It was a provocation—the wood had been paid for—and a party of five hundred men set out from Canudos to recover it. A hundred state police intercepted them, fired without warning and killed more than 150. The others fought back with sticks, iron bars, tree branches and a few old muskets. They drove off the police, who looted and burnt the settlement where it happened and arrived home after a four-day forced march, *their uniforms in shreds, wounded, crippled, exhausted.* The governor of Bahia telegrammed Rio for the federal government to intervene. The president of Brazil was sick and the vice president ordered five hundred troops to march on Canudos from Salvador. When the troops arrived in the outback in January 1897, with their fourteen officers and two small Krupp cannons, they found ten kilometers of scorched earth around Canudos. Not a building, not a tree. They marched into an ambush and after twelve hours of fighting retreated in confusion, fired on from the surrounding scrub on all sides by the Counselor's men.

Confusion overcame Rio too, where the young republic was being racked by its own troubles. The vice president was trying to force its first civilian leader from office, with the connivance of the military high command, who felt the president was too liberal, too close to the coffee growers. The Counselor had already got entangled in the power struggles of Bahia's ruling group and in Rio the military saw enemies everywhere. Coffee, the republic's main earner and the president's main support, was in free fall on the world commodity markets. Now the rumors of *monarchism* in Canudos set off a panic among the high command in Rio. From the capital, the movement at Canudos looked like an insurrection against the army's republican coup of seven years earlier and the army had just lost its opening skirmish. It was not a good moment to seem to be opting out of Brazil.

Antônio the Counselor was not unknown in Rio. Canudos had been settled barely more than a year when Machado de Assis made the Counselor and his followers the pretext for one of his urbanely inconsequential weekly magazine columns. The drylanders were exotic and remote enough to let Machado fantasize in his gracefully reassuring manner about the glamour—sexual and otherwise—of an outlaw band, which is what he vaguely took them to be. He deprecated by contrast the relentlessly modern metropolitan life of Rio, in a way that was sure to flatter and titillate his mainly female readers. Right from the start Canudos impinged on the mind of the capital, and right from the start the capital got it wrong, though Machado got it less wrong than others. He had kept his ironical distance from the institutions of the empire and he maintained it now from the convulsive enthusiasms of the republic. He wrote again about Canudos and the Counselor in January of 1897, while Rio was quivering with fascinated anger, whipped up by politicians and journalists, at the *fanatics* in the distant drylands who had just routed the nation's troops. As carefully light in touch as ever, but with a barely perceptible edge in his tone, Machado reminded his readers that in Rio they knew next to nothing about the people of Canudos or the Counselor, how they lived or what they believed. Since these people had now been living together—and fighting and dying together—in large numbers for several years, Machado suggested they might deserve some friendly attention. Provocatively—in the name of imagination and inclusiveness—he made oblique fun of the grimly positivist future being mapped out for Brazil. He imagined the Counselor as a colorful new addition to the parliament.

We'll lose all this by hunting him down. We'll end up over-thowing the apostle, destroying the sect and killing the fanatics. Peace will come back to the drylands and with it monotony. Monotony will come into our own minds again too. What will we have left when the law has won out?

Nobody listened to a novelist. Rio was in a political panic. Military and civilian powers turned from fighting each other to confront what they decided was a threat to the Brazilian republic's existence. Canudos had to be crushed. A new force of thirteen hundred men with artillery, cavalry and four cannons was assembled. Its commander was Colonel Moreira Cesar, a bandy-legged martinet who had first shown promise as a young officer when he murdered a journalist who had criticized the army. He had proven himself by crushing dissent in the military republic, and being without scruple he was thought just the man to eliminate Canudos.

Machado tried once again a couple of weeks later. *Yesterday I found out what celebrity is,* he wrote in mid-February. He had been buying a paper when a woman—a *simple* woman who he thought *didn't know how to read*—had asked the man in the kiosk for *a paper with a picture of the man who's out there fighting.* She couldn't

recall his name, but she meant the Counselor. Machado didn't
insist on the matter, and soon floated off into literary matters, but
the terms of the woman's recognition and the fact that she wanted
a picture of the Counselor carried their own freight, and so did
Machado's reminder to his metropolitan readers that the government's panic over the Counselor was sending Brazilian stocks
plummeting in London and New York. A fortnight after that
Machado gave up writing his weekly magazine column for good.

One of the things the landowners of Bahia's drylands were
always telling each other, and telling anyone who would listen
in Salvador and Rio, was that cattle thieves and criminals from
all over the interior were hiding out in Canudos. It was a lie—
the Counselor had an old-fashioned respect for private property
and Canudos did good business around the district—but there
were men in the Counselor's personal guard who had been in
trouble with the law. Not many people hadn't, in a region where
the judges served the landowners and the police were violent,
predatory and mostly uncontrolled. Banditry was on the rise all
through the Northeast, and former members of big bushranger
gangs—one of them wanted for eighteen murders in another
district—made the Canudos militia a formidable force. There
were eight hundred men in the Counselor's Catholic Guard, led
by the man who had fought off the police when they first tried
to kill the Counselor four years before. The *street commander* in
Canudos came from a *good family* and was a close friend of the
richest and most influential of the several merchants who did
business in town, a man who always wore a suit and tie and
practically ran the economy of Canudos—his notes of credit were
its currency. The merchant was also the man who imported,
stockpiled and distributed the weaponry. The militia leader and
the merchant were both unusually tall and about the only people
in Canudos who lived in big houses with tiled roofs. They were

dispensers of civil justice and the mainstays of civil order, the lay leaders of Canudos.

The Counselor had chosen Canudos with fine strategic instinct. It was the best place for water—from unseen artesian sources below ground and the river above—for miles around, and a site nobody could take by surprise. Ignoring the rout of the earlier expedition against it, Colonel Moreira Cesar sailed north from Rio in perfect confidence that his own much larger force would have no trouble against a settlement of unruly country people, and hardly bothered with the details of distance, climate, water, terrain in a region he knew nothing of. From Salvador he drove his men at a forced pace through the heat and desert of the drought. The transport wagons sank to the axle in sand, the soldiers tore their uniforms on the dense thorn shrub. At the expedition's first stop, engineers found they had brought the wrong equipment and were unable to sink a well for water. They had to press on.

As they neared Canudos and passed glowing embers from recent fires and remains of meals of roast kid and roast turtle, they realized their progress was being tracked by unseen eyes. They were drenched by a sudden downpour and everything turned to mud. Then the sun was blazing again. A group of horsemen galloped up and caused a panic, but they were guides sent by one of the landowners. They slept uneasily, the officers holding their horses' reins, and set off precipitously at first light. They were fired on near a homestead, but the attackers soon withdrew and the retreat gave the troops confidence. The colonel announced, *These people are unarmed* and urged his men on faster. He wanted to get in artillery range of Canudos. Morale soared. They were about to do what they had come to do. Under the scorching sun the troops scrambled up the slope of Monte Favella and on its peak they positioned the four Krupp cannons to fire on the settlement at its base. The size of the place quite startled them when they caught sight of Canudos below them, its thousands of small houses, the labyrinth of streets, the big square with the churches. The cannons started firing. A church bell below rang an alarm. Then the smoke from the cannons and the fires that broke out in the settlement and the dust raised by the smashed mud brick walls hid everything from sight. After a while the soldiers made out a scurrying of insect figures in the town, men heading into the scrub with rifles, women and children running for cover behind the thick walls of the unfinished new church. Nobody fired back and after a while the labyrinth of alleys was deserted again. The silence was total.

At one in the afternoon, under cover of artillery mounted on the hill across the river and facing the unfinished church, two columns of soldiers came down the slopes with their bayonets fixed. Buglers played as they crossed the river and entered the town, meeting only pebbles fired from ancient muskets. Then everything broke up. Inside the settlement the troops got lost in the maze of narrow irregular alleys. They were no longer a compact body but fighting as individuals against men who ambushed them with rifles, knives, scythes and table legs. The houses were solid. If grenades were used to blow them up, the rubble blocked advance. In the town, the soldiers lost the cover of their artillery, which could no longer fire without killing the men it was meant to protect. Snipers from the Catholic Guard hidden in the church tower picked off the military with impunity as the bell tolled again.

The colonel, who was starting to lose his nerve, ordered a cavalry charge, but the horses were spooked by the rifle fire coming across the river.

Darkness came quickly and after five hours of fighting the troops pulled out of the town. Now they were attacked from the scrub. The retreat turned into a rout. Platoons disintegrated as soldiers fought each other to escape, trampled the wounded, threw themselves into the river. The colonel, who was particularly loathed by his own men, fell from a bullet in the back. The people of Canudos gathered for the Angelus, and the troops could hear the Ave Maria drifting over the water as they hauled their cannons off. There were more than a hundred wounded beside the dying colonel, and they spent the night untreated, surrounded by the others, hidden in the darkness. The colonel refused a general retreat, but he was ignored and dead before daybreak. His men retreated without order, increasingly gripped by panic as the Canudos militia picked them off one by one from the scrub, dropping their weapons, their equipment and their wounded as they fled. They dumped the dead colonel, who was buried later with the others by the people of Canudos. The colonel who replaced him as leader was then himself killed in the retreat. At the end of the rout, the Canudos militia attacked the artillery and seized the army guns. The third expedition against Canudos had ended like the others.

Mud brick houses with one or two rooms, open spaces for doors and windows and dry fronds as a roof were soon rebuilt. Even after the assault by thirteen hundred troops with cannons, and although the governments of Bahia and Brazil were clearly determined to destroy the settlement, new people kept on coming to settle in Canudos. The Counselor was irresistibly attractive to the people struggling to survive in the interior. The balladeers of the drylands sang about him, and mocked the fallen Moreira Cesar. The landowners worked themselves into a frenzy about feared and rumored invasions of their property, attacks on their homesteads which never happened.

The people of Canudos knew nothing of the howling mobs that raged through the big cities after the army's new disaster in Canudos, and torched the offices of the monarchist press. They knew nothing of the national mourning decreed in Rio, the masses for the dead soldiers, the queues of volunteers from the *best families* lining up to join the forces of retribution. Without meaning to, the Counselor's subsistence farmers had shaken the republic to the point where the very future of Brazil was felt to depend on the total extermination of Canudos. As hard and canny veterans of dryland blood feuds, however, and victims of all the local agencies of power, they did know that bad brought worse and worse was coming. Canudos resumed its work on the big church—the Counselor was sixty-seven now, and anxious to see it finished soon—unknowing or uncaring that in the south they were seen as primitives, fanatics, a threat to civilization and the matter of other people's bad dreams. They had no idea that in London, having the benefit of distance, the *Times* sagely deemed the trouble insignificant in itself, but worried about the threat to the future stability of an outpost of the British economy. Brazil was finding itself unable to service its debt to the London banks.

After a while Canudos would have heard of the tumult in Salvador—the city on the coast was swollen now with soldiery and engineers and matériel. And of course the press. Men, armaments and war correspondents were shipped up from the south, banquets were held for the important visitors, Salvador's retail business flourished amid drunken brawls and sexual assaults. The entire Brazilian army was moving toward Canudos: thousands of troops from ten different states, with hundreds of machine guns, dozens of Krupp cannons, cavalry, engineers were gradually assembled in Salvador. Boys of thirteen were pressed into service to exterminate Canudos. It took more than three months to assemble the fourth expeditionary force. Over eight thousand men marched on Canudos that June, led by three generals and the minster for war himself, Marshal Bittencourt. Quite a few of the troops were recruited in the northeastern drylands, men who knew the terrain and its people. The new expedition was not going to make the mistakes of the last.

It was spooky all the same. Along the route they saw the rotting corpses of the men of the last expedition hanging from the thorn trees. The roadside was littered with skulls, and shreds of old army uniforms fluttered tangled in the thorns. One of the corpses they saw was the colonel who had led the retreat after the death of Moreira Cesar. Then a battalion was drawn into an ambush and hundreds of soldiers were killed. It was not beginning well. The expedition was being swept by rumors—reports that the Counselor's jagunços had taken surrounding towns, that foreign arms and mercenaries were getting to Canudos. The republican paranoia in Rio fed reports in the newspapers that the United States, France and Austria were ready to intervene and bring back the monarchy to Brazil. In Bahia, the drylanders' skill at moving unseen and fast around tracts of near desert fed the soldiers' panicky sense that they were facing an unknowable and invisible enemy. They were being attacked everywhere with the captured arms of the third expedition. Hundreds of soldiers deserted and made off into the scrub, and some of these joined the fighters from Canudos.

But the fourth expedition reached the district largely intact and set up its headquarters in the town of Monte Santo, throwing the inhabitants out of their houses to accommodate Marshal Bittencourt and the generals. The assault on Canudos began in July. Fifteen hundred men were dispatched to hold Monte Favella above Canudos, six thousand to surround the settlers and starve them. It took the army more than two months to lay a siege line around the settlement. In its first assault on Canudos the army lost a thousand men. Thereafter hundreds died each day among the army and the Canudos fighters from wounds or sickness. It went on for more than two months, and over time superior technology and the blockade on food and water began to tell. The dead were in their thousands and thousands. The fighters were able to slip out through the siege lines, and the battle of Canudos was fought as a series of guerrilla skirmishes over a wide area, but the center was always the settlement itself. The people never gave up.

Toward the end, some who had more to lose than their lives took stock. The merchant, who had moved to Canudos with his entire extended family, decided it was time to move on. He took leave of the Counselor, who was now sick with dysentery, and took his family away in small groups. He buried four boxes of silver in Canudos, and took with him several kilos of gold back to his home state of Ceará. On September 22 Antônio the Counselor died and was buried and two days later the army finally succeeded in encircling Canudos. Some of the fighters slipped away under cover of dark. The rest stayed. The jagunços counterattacked every night with their rifles—eighteen assaults on the night of September 27. On the first of October the army threw its heavy artillery at Canudos, smashing the mud brick houses where the inhabitants were sheltered and hurling grenades. Fires broke out and the whole settlement began to burn. Nobody cried out, nobody ran in the streets. They died silently in their homes.

The next day, being promised safety, five hundred women, some small children and a few old and wounded men gave themselves up to the army. The campaign photographer was brought over to take a picture of them huddled on the ground. The women's faces under shawls were masks of fear and pain, the children naked, the men grouped less distinctly at the back. The picture he took—unlike the endless studies of lines of tightly buttoned officers and wild eyed ragged soldiery he recorded standing outside their tents—came in close, at least to the women and children in the front, and the image of a mound of humanity was given a depth and strangely expressionist intensity by the flowing lines of the headcloths that framed the terrified fixity of the stares, all fenced in by the line of sticklike standing soldiers and a broken tree at the very back. When the photographer had done his work the military, notwithstanding their promise, cut the men to pieces under the women's eyes. The picture that survived was not technically remarkable, which was hardly surprising in the circumstances. It was greatly overexposed and seemed to obliterate its dreadful secrets just as an observer's ravenous horrified eye closed in on the detail. The foreground faces and figures that remained spoke for the others that were lost in the short distance. The drearily competent war photographer Flávio de Barros was probably unaware that he had caught one of the great images of the horrors of modern war, the first war photograph that registered not the combatants, bearded, male, alive or dead—and Barros brought back from Canudos nothing like the North American Civil War photographs taken by Mathew Brady decades earlier—but the collaterally damaged, the women, the children, the old, the hurt, frozen on their brief passage from one horror to a worse. The bleached out picture cast its shadow forward to certain images caught in Central Europe nearly half a century later.

In Brazil, it would not be matched until Sebastião Salgado published his photographs of the immense open gold mine of Serra Pelada nearly a hundred years later. Salgado's panoramic photographs were Dantescan: as images of an obscure punishment from which there was no escape, no end in sight, they would have seemed monstrous imaginings had they not been so precisely and unfakeably what they were. The mud of Serra Pelada had its continuities with the stone and grit of Canudos. A century on, the desperation of the Brazilian poor in the remotest corners of the country had found a new setting and no solution. Serra Pelada is worse: its miners have not been exterminated but—working their individual claims amid the arbitrary violence of their neighbors and the police—they have never known solidarity, never realized the beginnings of a shared future. Observers at Canudos described from their vantage point how the people died *like ants* under the army's final cannonade, a killing force that came from outside. Salgado's image shows people dying *like ants* without the intervention of the army.

The jagunços made their last stand firing from a trench by the Counselor's unfinished church. Among them were the last two chiefs of the Kiriri índios. The last to fall under the fire of five thousand infantry were an old man, two fighting men and a boy. No male of any age survived the destruction of Canudos. Every male prisoner, man or child, was taken out into the thorn scrub by the republican forces and his throat was slit. Many were treated worse. Prisoners had their eyes gouged out, were cut to pieces, children were smashed against trees. The army counted over five thousand houses in Canudos, and then dynamited and torched all those which had survived bombardment and fire, along with the thousands of unburied bodies of their inhabitants. There was a frenzy to eliminate every trace of the place and its inhabitants.

But there were too many dead. Fifteen thousand or more from the last days. Clouds of carrion birds hung in the air over Canudos and dogs howled for their fallen owners on the ground. For years afterward, whenever rains came, corpses washed up, mummified in the desert air and still dressed, some of them, in their officers' blue republican uniforms with the red stripe. Year after year after year, every little drylands shower brought up skulls and bones that the hooves of the oxen and the mules slowly ground back into the quartz and granite. The frenzy of extermination did not allow the Counselor to lie in peace. Two days after his community was razed, the army discovered where Antônio Vicente Mendes Maciel was buried and they dug him up and photographed the corpse. The picture of the dead and bearded Counselor anticipated the postmortem photographs of the bearded Che Guevara taken in Bolivia seventy years later.

They hacked off the decomposing head with a knife and carried it on a pike in civilization's victory parade through Salvador, much as Zumbi's had been after the destruction of Palmares two hundred years before. Then, this being the age of science, the head was taken to the Medical Faculty of Bahia to be studied for *abnormalities.*

When the troops arrived back in Rio the president went to meet them at the docks, and during the victory parade an ensign tried to assassinate him. The war minister Bittencourt stepped forward to help the president and was himself stabbed to death instead. Whether it was a conspiracy by the military was never known: the ensign's death in prison several weeks later was reported as suicide. Civilian rule tottered on. The nineteenth century was ending and Brazil was deeper in debt than ever to Britain, America, France, Germany. The war against Canudos nearly bankrupted the nation.

———

Traveling to Canudos now from Salvador, you go over paved roads over what seems for most of the way a straight line. The road just rises gently into terrain that is ever more sparsely peopled and trees and grass are gradually replaced by thorn scrub and spiky succulents, the cars by trucks and mules and bicycles. The journey from Salvador that Brazilian troops made over several days I did by bus in eleven hours. The railway was no more but the roads had improved. I left before daybreak and the light was still gray when the roadside monotony was broken by what looked like a vast and very trim military encampment. Hundreds of small structures were laid out in rows and rows of dead straight lines. They caught the eye because they were bright black and yellow. Wooden frames were walled in shiny black plastic sheeting and roofed in fresh straw. I assumed it was the army encamped here, but the big flag on the pole by the gate